# Marco Polo

## THE STORY OF THE FASTEST CLIPPER

## MARTIN J. HOLLENBERG

## NIMBUS
PUBLISHING

*⌐ꙅ J or Button ꙅ⌐*

Nimbus Publishing Limited
PO Box 9166, Halifax, NS B3K 5M8
(902) 455-4286

Printed and bound in Canada

Design: John van der Woude
Front cover: Painting of the *Marco Polo* by John Lars Johnson, c.1930. Courtesy of the New Brunswick Museum (20898).
Author photo: Kingdom Photo Ltd, Vancouver

The lyrics of "We Built This Old Ship" by Jim Stewart and Gordon Bok are reprinted by permission of Jim Stewart. © 1988 Jim Stewart & Gordon Bok, SOCAN.
The lyrics of "Marco Polo" by Hughie Jones are reprinted by permission of Hughie Jones and Harmony Music. © Harmony Music.

Library and Archives Canada Cataloguing in Publication

    Hollenberg, Martin
    Marco Polo : the story of the fastest clipper / Martin Hollenberg.
    Includes bibliographical references and index.
    ISBN 1-55109-565-3

1. Marco Polo (Ship)—History. 2. Clipper ships—Canada—History—19th century. 3. Clipper ships—Australia—History—19th century. 4. Voyages around the world. 5. Australia—Emigration and immigration—History—19th century. I. Title.

G420.M37H64 2006    910.4'1    C2006-901496-5

Published in the United Kingdom and Europe by: Chatham Publishing, an imprint of Lionel Leventhal Ltd, Park House, 1 Russell Gardens, London NW11 9NN
UK ISBN-10: 1-86176-297-6
UK ISBN-13: 978-86176-297-9

We acknowledge the financial support of the Government of Canada through the Book Publishing Industry Development Program (BPIDP) and the Canada Council, and of the Province of Nova Scotia through the Department of Tourism, Culture and Heritage for our publishing activities.

# CONTENTS

# ACKNOWLEDGEMENTS

*I* gratefully acknowledge the support of the University of British Columbia, and in particular its library and my home Department of Anatomy (now a division of the Department of Cellular and Physiological Sciences). I am also deeply indebted to Tony Arseneau and Jim Stewart of Saint John, New Brunswick, who helped in many ways, especially by sharing with me their knowledge of *Marco Polo* and its story. Our very good friends, Nancy and Gerry Wright of London, Ontario, did essential research for the book in the libraries of Australia. Benjamin Singer of the University of Western Ontario and Charles Roland of McMaster Univeristy provided invaluable help in editing the manuscript. As well, I am deeply indebted to many people throughout the world who generously allowed me to include in the book quotations and illustrations from their work. Special credit and thanks are also due to The Archives Office of Tasmania, State Library of Victoria, Melbourne, National Library of Australia, Canberra, State Library of New South Wales, Sydney and the National Museums Liverpool (Merseyside Maritime Museum) for sharing with me copies of letters and diaries written by passengers on *Marco Polo*, as well as copies of *The Marco Polo Chronicle*.

I am most grateful also to Sandra McIntyre, James MacNevin, and Heather Bryan of Nimbus Publishing, who provided key editorial assistance and helped me guide the book through the many phases of the publishing process. They never wavered in their support and enthusiasm for the book.

Finally, I extend my thanks and love to my family: Button, Andy and Kris, Myles and Drew, and Lesley and Peter. They never missed an opportunity to ask, "When will the book be out?"

**Figure 1** This painting by the late Jack Koskie shows *Marco Polo* arriving in Port Phillip Bay. Its sails are being furled as a steam-driven, paddle-wheel tug approaches. Like other merchant ships of its time, it had "gun ports" painted on its planking to make it more interesting and add a bit of romance to its appearance. It flies the Black Ball flag at its main, its identifying code at its mizzen, and the British red ensign behind.

# INTRODUCTION

The day after Christmas, 1852, the Black Ball clipper *Marco Polo* arrived back at the Salthouse Dock in Liverpool, England, to the absolute astonishment of all. On its arrival, the captain and crew mounted a boldly printed banner between the fore- and mainmasts that read, "The Fastest Ship in the World." It had just completed the round-the-world voyage to Melbourne and back in the unheard-of time of five months and twenty-one days, including a layover in Melbourne of twenty-four days. Prior to that, no ship driven by wind or steam or both had circumnavigated the globe in less than six months. In fact, at that time, the average one-way trip from Liverpool to Melbourne took about 110 days and from London to Melbourne about ten days longer. *Marco Polo*'s early arrival caused a sensation. In the ensuing days, enthusiasts from all over the British Isles crowded the Liverpool docks to catch a glimpse of this great vessel. Almost overnight, *Marco Polo* and its builder and owners became famous, and the Black Ball Line became renowned for the speed and carrying capacity of its ships on the Australian passage.

Why was *Marco Polo* so fast? Perhaps it was the design and construction, which were so unusual for a clipper that some found it ugly, or its ability to carry a full spread of canvas in gales that may have damaged or even destroyed other ships. It could have been the captain's use of US Naval Lieutenant Maury's charts of winds and currents, and the new great circle route to Australia, or the ability to calculate the longitude accurately and frequently using sextants and reliable chronometers set to Greenwich time. Or perhaps it was the captain himself, the hard-driving, irascible James Nicol "Bully" Forbes, who allegedly told a group of passengers frightened by bad weather that his uncompromising goal was "Hell or Melbourne." In the final analysis,

was *Marco Polo* really "The Fastest Ship in the World," as its captain
and crew claimed?

From its construction at Marsh Creek near Saint John, New
Brunswick, in 1850–51, to its deliberate wreckage onto the shore to
save crew and cargo in 1883, the life story of this ship is a full and
extraordinary one. The remarkable group of people who built, owned,
sailed, and travelled aboard is no small part of the *Marco Polo* story.
Four of the most interesting individuals in the history of the merchant
marine are directly involved: James Smith, a Canadian builder; James
Baines and Thomas Miller Mackay, *Marco Polo's* principal British owners; and James Nicol Forbes, the captain on the ship's first two record-
breaking, round-the-world voyages from Liverpool to Melbourne and
back. Threats of disease on board the ship, efforts to preserve the health
of the passengers, and the limited capabilities of the medicine of that
period compared to today are also examined by way of *Marco Polo's*
accomplishments.

The ship became famous during a period that included the mid-nineteenth century shipbuilding boom in British North America and the
United States, the Australian gold rush in the 1850s, and the mass exodus
through Liverpool to Australia of gold seekers and others escaping poverty, hunger, and oppression in Europe. *Marco Polo* spent fifteen years
as a passenger ship on the Australian run with the Black Ball Line (from
1852–67), made close to twenty-five round-trip voyages during that
period (averaging about five every three years), and carried nearly fifteen
thousand passengers to the new land. Projecting from this total, perhaps
as many as a million Australians today are descended from the original
group carried by this famous ship from Liverpool to Melbourne.

Since its birth on Marsh Creek, *Marco Polo* has been celebrated in
song, especially by the people of New Brunswick. These refrains give
us a different perspective of the ship and the men who built and sailed
it. "We Built This Old Ship," a 1988 composition by Jim Stewart and
Gordon Bok, portrays the sentiment of the ship's builders. It has become
one of the most popular of the *Marco Polo* songs.

> *We gathered the tamarack, oak, birch and pine*
> *We took from the forest and took to the shore*
> *And we gave her her breath and her strength and her line*
> *With the skills we had learned from our fathers before*

*We worked in the rain and the heat and the cold*
*We cursed and rejoiced in our pride and our pain*
*And we never imagined our hands would grow old*
*And her like on the water we'd not see again*

Chorus
*We built this old ship with our sweat and endeavour*
*She ran with the wind and the wind set her free*
*And we once dared to dream she would sail on forever*
*But although she was ours she belonged to the sea.*

There can be no doubt that *Marco Polo* was a clipper ship with a remarkable history that brought grief and joy—and sometimes both—to many people on three continents. Simply, *Marco Polo* was one of the most unusual and famous ships that ever sailed.

# A New Brunswick Clipper is Born

*"The never-to be-forgotten sounds of those lovely summer mornings still ring in my ears. The sharp 'click' of the fastener's mall as the bolts were secured, the loud and merry ring of the caulker's mallet, the 'thub, thub' of the dubber's adze, the muffled blows on treenails, the swishing of broad axes, the whining saws, the hissing, spluttering steambox when the steamed planks were withdrawn, combined in a jubilation of shipyard noises."*
—Christina Ross Frame, Maitland, Nova Scotia, 1927

## Shipbuilding in the Maritime Provinces in the Nineteenth Century

*I*n the middle decades of the nineteenth century, the Canadian Maritime Provinces—Prince Edward Island, Nova Scotia, and New Brunswick—became major shipbuilding centres. Never before (or since) had there been such activity in this area of the world in the construction of wooden sailing ships. In almost every river and stream, ships were being built.

All the essentials for a highly productive shipbuilding industry were in place. There was a plentiful supply of lumber from thick forests that often grew close to the water's edge. There were remarkably skilled shipwrights and other marine craftsmen newly arrived from western Europe, especially the British Isles. Local descendants of United Empire Loyalists, used to working in wood on the farm, were present and some, in time, became major ship owners. As well, during most of this period, the tariffs and naval regulations in Britain were favourable to Canadian builders, and there were eager markets on both sides of the Atlantic for the ships' products, especially timber. Even the wooden ships themselves were readily marketable. At its shipbuilding peak in the mid–1800s, Maritime Canada ranked near the top on the roster of the world's leading ship-owning regions. Certain productive ports, such as Saint John and Yarmouth, became widely recognized as great centres of commerce and shipbuilding activity.

Demand was high for Canadian wooden ships for several reasons. There was a desperate need for ships to transport miners and prospectors from the eastern United States to the California gold rush of 1848–49 and from Britain to the Australian gold rush, in 1851. Also, there was an urgent requirement in Britain for ships to supply the Crimean War of 1854–56, and to carry large numbers of new settlers from Britain to North America, Australia, and New Zealand. A lack of competition from east coast shipyards in America during the American Civil War of 1861–65 aided Canadian shipbuilders as well.

Many different types of wooden sailing vessels were built to carry both people and cargo. These included large, full-rigged ships with three masts and square sails, barques, barquentines, and two-masted brigs and brigantines. Small vessels such as sloops and cutters appeared in abundance for fishing, coasting, and local commerce. The use of fore-and-aft instead of rectangular sails on some of the masts of these vessels reduced the number of crew members needed, and allowed them to sail closer to the wind. Fishing schooners, sometimes used for racing, were also built in Maritime Canada during this period, and for years afterwards as well. These would be the precursors to the celebrated *Bluenose*. Launched on March 26, 1921, at Lunenburg, Nova Scotia, and made of Nova Scotian spruce, oak, birch, and pine, the sleek and powerful *Bluenose* was destined to become a champion—world-famous for its speed, beauty, and magnificent sailing capabilities.

Shipbuilding in the nineteenth century was carried out on a massive scale. Throughout the Maritimes, close to ten thousand wooden vessels were built during the 1800s. In New Brunswick alone (with a population in 1871 of only 285,594), over one thousand new ships were registered between 1825 and 1870. The number of new ships registered at Saint John peaked in the 1850s, with most built from 1830 to 1860. During those years, the construction of wooden sailing ships became the foremost manufacturing enterprise in the

Maritimes, and many enduring companies and family shipbuilding histories were created.

Timber became the principal export throughout the Maritimes and the amount of lumber exported to England grew a thousand fold, from almost a thousand tons in 1808 to more than a million tons in 1847. Manufactured goods—including intricate parts for ships such as pumps, binnacles, and capstans—were transported in the opposite direction, from Britain to its North American colonies. Of course, thousands of emigrants were transported as well. Accommodating this exchange required more than one fifth of all British registered tonnage. As well, an active trade of various goods took place between the colonies of British North America and the nearby eastern seaports of the United States, and lumber and fish were shipped from North America to the West Indies in return for sugar, rum, and molasses.

To carry loads of local timber, square-rigged ships with large, capacious holds were produced in the Canadian Maritimes in the 1800s. Although speed was a secondary consideration during their construction, a number of these ships turned out to be bigger and faster than their British-built merchantman counterparts. A few special ones were destined to establish world records. These ships were generally considered inferior by ship owners in England because—unlike the British ships—they were built mainly from softwoods like spruce, pine, and tamarack (also called hackmatack, American larch, cypress or juniper) rather than hardwoods like oak and teak. Moreover, their interiors were not as elaborately finished. Typically, for insurance purposes, Lloyds of London, the maritime insurance giant, would assign a high rating (A1) to the best of these Canadian-built softwood vessels, anticipating that some would remain in service for decades, despite strain and waterlogging. In truth, the lifespan of vessels varied wildly—some sailed on the high seas for three decades or more; others became unfit to sail after transporting timber for only one or two seasons.

The usual practice at that time in New Brunswick and the rest of the Maritimes was to construct each ship locally in one of the major Canadian shipbuilding yards, load it with timber, then sail it immediately to a British port, where both the lumber in the ship's hold and the ship itself would be offered for sale. To handle the ships on their long voyages, a hard-working and reliable crew was trained over the decades. Many of these Canadian "Bluenose" seamen worked their way up to become second mates, mates, and even master mariners (captains), at a surprisingly young age. They were rough and ready, extremely capable, and trained to a high standard. They may not have been experts in the mathematics of navigation, but they knew the sea and their ships well, and could reach any port on the globe with surprising accuracy. They soon earned an enviable, worldwide reputation.

Towards the end of the nineteenth century, the number of ships built in the Maritime Provinces declined precipitously. As competition for load, durability, and speed increased, shipping firms switched from wooden, wind-driven ships to iron-hulled, steam-propelled vessels, built mainly in the British Isles. Regrettably, few Canadian shipwrights of the period had the skills to work in iron or steel. Shipbuilding in Canada rapidly became a minor industry—a craft even, despite the fact that Canada's overall economy was expanding dramatically at the time. As well, plates of these metals were very expensive in Canada. Britain, in contrast, had the industrial infrastructure to produce iron- and steel-hulled vessels in large numbers whether they were propelled by sail or by steam. This shift spelled the end of the glory years of the Canadian wooden shipbuilding industry. The conclusion of a magnificent era in the new country's history was at hand. No more would the sounds of ships being built fill Canadian Maritime waterways and forests.

Today, the modern world has taken over and one would have to search painstakingly to find evidence of the once-numerous Canadian shipyards, where so many great wooden vessels were built and the craft of so many talented shipwrights practised. The artistry of these highly skilled shipwrights can be found only in museums now, and in the few remaining houses, churches, and other buildings they built.

## Saint John, New Brunswick

Similarly, museums and historical documents are all we have to help us understand what it must have been like to live and work in the great Canadian shipbuilding centres of that time. Of those, perhaps none was more interesting or active than Saint John, New Brunswick.

Strategically located where the Saint John River flows into the Bay of Fundy, Saint John was bound on its landward side by many active shipyards. Within the busy port city itself, an infrastructure of trades and

**Figure 2** Saint John harbour in the days of sail. All loading and unloading of the sailing vessels had to be done by hand or with simple lifting aids. Horses and wagons were used extensively on the docks to transport cargo to and from the ships.

**Figure 3** Saint John harbour circa 1898, as seen from Chubb's Corner on Prince William Street.

shops designed to support the shipbuilding industry gradually developed over the century. These included stores and warehouses selling imported ship fittings, sail and rigging repairers and manufacturers, block and pump makers, caulkers, ship chandlers, and iron founders. Carvers and guilders of the picturesque figureheads that adorned the bows of most major sailing vessels worked alongside tradesmen highly skilled in carving fancy scrollwork; such tradesmen also made tables and other furnishings for the ships' interiors.

No description of Saint John in the nineteenth century would be complete without mention of Cody's coffee house. The Exchange Coffee House in Saint John was established by William George Cody in 1803. For decades it acted as a key gathering place, where the leading citizens of the city could meet socially as well as transact business related to their shipping and other commercial interests.

## James Smith, Builder of *Marco Polo*

Many superb shipwrights were working in New Brunswick during the nineteenth century, and, fortunately, many of their biographies— including descriptions of the ships they built—have been recorded by several dedicated Maritime writers. These accounts nearly always mention a handsome, clean-shaven, intense, and determined young man by the name of James Smith. Called "Fortune's plaything" by Esther Clark Wright, author of *Saint John Ships and Their Builders,* Smith was a well-known, innovative and prolific shipbuilder who had a fascinating, turbulent career.

James Smith was born into a military family on the island of Guernsey in the summer of 1802, although the family home was near Monaghan, Northern Ireland. His mother, a McDonald, died when he was only ten, and one of his brothers was killed at the battle of Waterloo, in 1815. His father was also at Waterloo, and earlier, at the Battle of Copenhagen; he survived both conflicts but did not maintain a home for young James, even after his army service was completed. As a result, James grew up in the home of an uncle.

When he was about seventeen, Smith left Ireland to seek his fortune in North America, accompanied by his cousin, James McDonald. The two arrived at Grand Falls, New Brunswick, and worked in the woods for a year or two felling white pine trees. Unfortunately, McDonald died about this time. Smith moved from Grand Falls to Saint John to further his career by working in shipyards. He quickly acquired a variety of woodworking skills and much invaluable knowledge about how large wooden sailing ships were built—skills and knowledge that would serve him well later.

At the age of about twenty-five, James Smith married Margaret McMorran, born in County Down, Ireland, and they had seven children. Within a few years of their marriage, tragedy struck and three of the children, aged eight, six, and four, died within a month of each other, probably from one of the highly contagious illnesses common at the time, such as diphtheria. Though none of James and Margaret's offspring survived past 1863, they did leave a number of descendants.

In 1836, Smith completed his apprenticeship and was admitted a freeman of Saint John, a kind of honorary citizenship that came with voting and other privileges, usually bestowed on men of property. His active ship-building career, which was to last close to twenty years, was officially underway. From 1836 to 1842, he and his crews built a number of ships for several owners. After that, Smith himself became both builder and owner of all the ships constructed by his crews, and he took on his eldest son, James, as partner.

**Figure 4** James Smith, "an honest man and an honest builder," conceived and designed *Marco Polo* and led the construction of the ship in 1850–51.

By 1850, Smith and his son had built eighteen large sailing ships, mainly cargo ships. Several were timber carriers, built in the hopes that they could be sold quickly to shipping firms in Liverpool or elsewhere. Smith's business was increasingly successful and he became quite prosperous, with two big homes and an interest in mining as well. His reputation soared; in Liverpool he became admired as an honest man and an honest builder. Then, at the peak of his success, James Smith built one ship that would overshadow them all.

## James Smith and Clipper Ship Design

In order to be competitive, Smith had to keep abreast of the latest developments in the design and construction of large sailing ships. To this end, he regularly visited shipyards in England, Scotland, the Canadian Maritimes and the eastern seaboard states. Despite the fact that the fundamental structure of the wind-driven ship had remained unchanged for close to four hundred years, improvements were constantly appearing and new knowledge was crucial. The height of James Smith's success coincided with the apex of the brief but splendid period of the clippers ships, and Smith, no doubt, knew of the new designs incorporated into these remarkable vessels. Few ships have excited so much interest as the clippers, celebrated then and now by people everywhere for their speed, grace, and beauty. The era of the clipper ship extended from about 1840 to 1875, the most active years for construction being from 1853 to 1855 in Britain and 1851 to 1854 in America. Many types were built, including China clippers, California clippers, tea clippers, coffee clippers, and opium clippers.

The exact definition of a clipper ship has varied over the years from one maritime writer to another. However, at the time they were built, the designation "clipper" was liberally applied to almost any large, fast, sailing ship built with at least some structural refinements favouring speed over carrying capacity. Such a designation was eagerly sought by ship owners since it could mean higher fees for faster delivery of cargo and passengers. This was just as well since clippers, in general, required larger crews to sail them and were expensive to operate.

There are three main classes of clipper ships: extreme clippers, clippers, and medium or half clippers. Extreme clippers, of which there are several types, were the fastest. Built almost exclusively between

1845 and 1855, extreme clippers were usually long and narrow, with a sharp entrance, a clean run, and a hull shaped like that of a large yacht. They were produced for only a decade because with limited carrying capacity and high operating costs, they could make money only when freight rates were at their peak. One of the most famous of the China tea clippers (even though it achieved faster passages when engaged in the Australian wool trade) is *Cutty Sark*. One glance at *Cutty Sark* is enough to register its beauty and grace, and explain why extreme clipper ships attracted so much attention and became so famous.

Clippers, in contrast to extreme clippers, have a fuller midsection and subsequently a larger cargo and passenger capacity. Still unusually graceful in appearance, especially when under full sail, they were able to operate at a profit with freight rates at moderate levels. With a good captain, they could equal extreme clippers in speed.

Medium or half clipper are terms reserved for general cargo or passenger vessels designed with an unusually sharp bow, a fair run, towering masts, and a broad, spacious hull amidships. Medium clippers were built mainly from 1845 to 1860, usually with a more streamlined appearance below the waterline than their non-clipper, merchantman, counterparts. Also, many wooden medium clippers were massively built and could remain stable and withstand considerable ocean pounding even when sailed at high speeds in rough weather. For these reasons, the rather plain-looking medium clippers became a practical alternative to the clippers or extreme clippers. Some, when driven especially hard, were even capable of achieving record times on long voyages, despite their bulk.

No doubt James Smith carefully considered the performance and appearance of various types of clippers and non-clippers alike while conceiving the best design for his new ship. Of prime importance was his desire to build a truly great ship, and one with a high profit potential that would sell quickly in the Liverpool market. In those times, that meant a large, square-rigged ship, with a capacious hull that could carry an enormous load of lumber or other valuable cargo. Smith perhaps also felt that the ship would have more potential should it be able to convert with a minimum of expense into a passenger-carrying packet ship. Speed, no doubt, was also a major consideration in Smith's planning, especially if the ship was to carry many passengers over vast distances. To accommodate such criteria, the ship would need the hull of a clipper ship modified to carry unusually large loads, as well as a massive wooden structure both below and above the waterline so it could sail hard, steady, and fast in the heaviest of seas.

In the end, Smith likely decided upon a medium clipper because it combined the best of all possibilities—a ship that could carry a full load of timber or passengers at an efficient rate of speed over long distances. Matching enormous depth and carrying capacity with flat floors and short, sharp ends would create the ideal ship for either the timber or the passenger trade. Whether or not Smith actually referred to his design as a medium clipper is hard to say; in 1850, medium clippers, so designated, had been sailing for only a few years. However, other, smaller merchant vessels possessing unusually sharp ends and graceful and sleek hulls had been built prior to 1850, and Smith may well have been influenced by the design of these smaller ships.

## BUILDING MARCO POLO

James Smith's shipyard was located near Saint John, New Brunswick, on a plot of land that sloped gently down to Marsh Creek. Today, the shipyard site is at Hanover and Crown streets in Saint John. In James Smith's time, Marsh Creek at low tide had little water in it and was a marshy, dank, and unattractive place, but at high tide it filled up enough to float a large vessel and carry it down to the sea at Courtenay Bay. In the yard adjoining Smith's, competitor shipwrights William and Richard Wright and their crews were at work on a rival vessel named *Beejapore*. It was to be the largest ship yet constructed in the region, with a length of 182 feet, three decks, and a half-poop. James Smith, always competitive, likely determined that his next ship would be just a little bit bigger than *Beejapore*. Probably to emphasize its ability to travel the world, he named it *Marco Polo*, after the famous Venetian traveller on the Silk Road to China. Not much more is known about the details of the construction of *Marco Polo*.

Smith's yard was likely rectangular in outline and probably contained a few large sheds housing an inventoried assortment of lumber, of lengths both straight and curved. There would have been a cookhouse and a blacksmith shop to provide the ships' iron fittings and fastenings. A wood-fired steam box or chest designed to render planks pliable for curving to the hull would also have been necessary. Sleeping quarters for James Smith, his foreman, and their workers might have been on the site as well. With no power of any kind in the yard, with the possible exception of a steam-driven sawmill, all cutting, shaping, joining, and hauling of lumber had to be done by the crew members themselves, using blocks and tackles, sheerlegs and other similar hoisting aids. Upwards of fifty talented shipwrights and a number of apprentices would have worked on *Marco Polo* at any one time, all engaged in a shipbuilding effort coordinated down to the last detail by Smith, "the Master," and John Fredrickson, his foreman.

To permit the lengthwise sawing of logs on site would have required either a sawpit hollowed out in the ground, or a sawing platform built above ground on sawhorses. If there was one, the sawpit would have been situated at the top of the yard away from Marsh Creek to keep it above the water table. Lined with planks and deep enough for a worker to stand upright in it, the sawpit was in daily use in most New

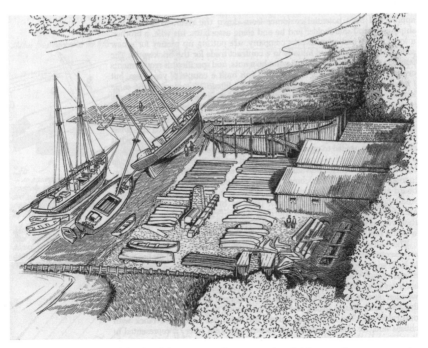

**Figure 5**  A shipyard for building wooden vessels, similar to the one used for *Marco Polo*. Note the vessel under construction (above) and the sawpit (lower right).

Brunswick shipyards at the time, even though timber, sawn into shape, was also available from local sawmills powered by wind, running water, or even steam. The logs to be shaped in the yard were hauled to the pit and hoisted over it using simple leveraging aids. Two workers, one on top of the log and one in the pit, combined their efforts by manning a rip saw with a handle at each end. The more experienced of the two directed the saw accurately from the favoured position above while his partner in the pit, usually an apprentice, pushed and pulled the saw while contending with both its weight and a continuous shower of sawdust. After a few seasons in the sawpit, apprentices were more than ready to leave it, and move up a notch in the hierarchy.

*Marco Polo*, like all wooden ships of the period, was built using the traditional hand tools owned by the shipwrights themselves, as well as some more specialized pieces of machinery owned by the yard, such as large hoisting rigs. Shipwrights' tools, similar to carpenter tools, included a variety of handsaws, an assortment of axes and adzes, many different types of chisels, hand and draw planes, and augers of all sizes. Almost certainly, a great deal of time was spent by crew members refashioning these tools and keeping them sharp—all knew that the secret to a good job was to use the correct tools, well-sharpened, in the right way. An assortment of hammers and mallets was also needed for many tasks, such as driving iron spikes and stout wooden pegs called treenails. Other specialized tools used for caulking included irons, oakum hooks, and scrapers. Shipwrights also used carpenters' compasses, folding rules, and plumb lines, but none of the instruments of the draftsman, nor his detailed plans.

Construction on *Marco Polo* began in James Smith's yard in the fall of 1850. This was an unusual time of year to start; most shipbuilding crews in the Canadian Maritimes in the 1800s spent their winters in the woods, felling trees and hauling them over the snow on sleds to sawmills or directly to shipyards. Smith's crew must have had lumber left over from ships built earlier, so they were able to proceed without spending time and energy cutting and hauling trees. This also meant, however, that they were prepared to build the ship outdoors through the cold Maritime winter.

After much planning about the overall contours and dimensions of *Marco Polo*, work commenced on its half-model. This crucial step was almost certainly taken by James Smith himself, working with his foreman, John Fredrickson. Today, prior to construction of a ship, naval architects produce multiple drawings and digitize them on computers so that the ship and its components can be viewed in three dimensions and from all angles. In the 1850s, plans or line drawings were rarely used; a tri-dimensional view of the ship's hull was obtained by fashioning a model of one half of the ship as if it were sectioned vertically from bow to stern in its midline. A model of the entire hull was not required since the ships were bilaterally symmetrical. The half-model was usually carved with a drawknife and spokeshave to a scale of one-quarter inch or three-eighths inch to the foot. The carving was done carefully and minutely since measurements, lines and curvatures taken from the half-model, scaled up, would guide construction of key components of the full-sized vessel, especially its frame skeleton. The model's outer dimensions corresponded to the outer surface of the ship's skeleton, rather than that of its external skin of planks. This exact conformity of the frames permitted forming the skeleton of the full-sized ship from the dimensions and shape of the half-model.

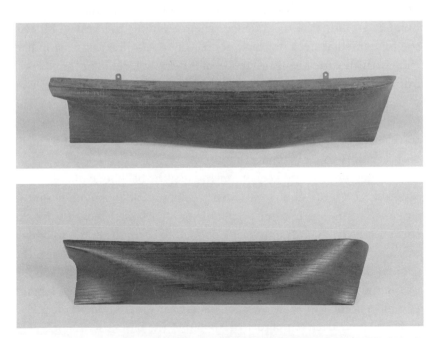

**Figures 6 & 7** The original half-model of *Marco Polo*, now in the Mariners' Museum, Newport News, Virginia. Its bow lies to the right.

Half-models were either carved from a solid block of softwood such as yellow pine, or, as in the case of *Marco Polo*, fashioned from a block formed by narrow, horizontal layers of wood held tightly together with vertical dowels. With the dowels removed, each layer of the fully carved, laminated block could be examined separately. The half-model was carefully measured in a room called the moulding loft, through a step-by-step process involving the making of thin wooden moulds scaled up to full size. The mathematical scales on a draftsman's rule were used to help calculate the exact dimensions for each mould. Under the drafts-man's guidance, the moulds were then used as templates or patterns for the construction of components such as frames, stem and sternposts.

Fortunately, the half-model of *Marco Polo* has survived and can be viewed at the Mariner's Museum in Newport News, Virginia. This lam-inated model, held together by dowels, shows a vessel with sharp ends and a full, rounded hull amidships. Definitely not pretty to look at, the model reveals a ship that, for its time, would have had a huge carrying capacity for lumber or people.

Rapid progress was made on *Marco Polo* over the winter of 1850–51. Smith's crew was highly experienced and followed a familiar and time-honoured construction sequence when building the vessel. Indeed, the fundamental steps involved in creating a wooden sailing ship had changed little since the introduction of the ship's skeleton or framework, hundreds of years earlier. For centuries prior, ships were built simply by constructing a shell of planks joined tightly together at their edges. The presence of a framework under the outer layer of planks, and fastened to the planks, was a fundamental improvement that added much strength and versatility to the overall structure.

The massive, straight keel of *Marco Polo*, the backbone of the vessel, was laid on a series of huge wooden blocks probably ascending up the slope of Smith's yard in a line perpendicular to Marsh Creek. The blocks (or collectively, stocks) were strong enough to carry the entire weight of the ship and high enough to permit work to be done underneath it. The ground under the blocks was probably compacted to prevent sinking or sliding. The keel was formed from sturdy, specially selected lengths of timber joined in such a way as to give it great strength. The keel may well have been temporarily fastened to the blocks so that it would remain straight and true throughout the construction process. Then, the sturdily constructed stem was bolted to the foremost portion of the

**Figure 8** This drawing shows the initial stages in construction of a wooden ship like *Marco Polo*. The keel has been laid on the blocks and the stem can be seen protruding upwards and securely fastened to the keel in the distance. In the foreground, shipwrights are fastening the sternpost to the keel with the aid of a hoisting device (sheerleg).

keel, and the massive sternposts to its opposite end. These components were fastened to the keel at the proper angle, or slant, for the bow and stern respectively. In anticipation of launching, almost certainly the keel was placed so that the stern of the completed ship, rather than its bow, would lie closest to Marsh Creek.

While work was underway on the keel, stem, and stern-posts, other crew members were busy fashioning the numerous frames which, when placed parallel to each other and crosswise to the keel, would form the vessel's skeleton. Each of the frames was scarphed together from several pieces of wood. Most were roughly u-shaped and designed to be firmly bolted to the keel at the bottom of the u. The frames were separated from each other on the keel by a narrow gap and were placed along the entire length of the ship. The outer surfaces of the frames were bevelled by hand to conform to lines taken from the half-model. In that way, the shape of the hull of the full-sized ship would correspond closely to that of the half-model, although some liberty in shaping the frames was probably taken.

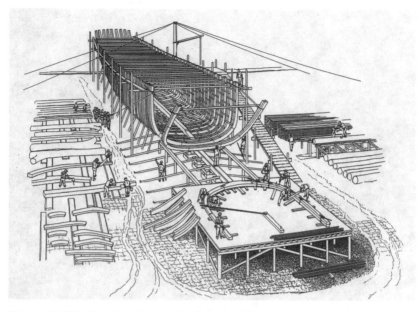

**Figure 9** This drawing shows the framing process used at the time *Marco Polo* was built. Note that the frames were assembled on the ground and then hoisted into position with the transverse beams.

**Figure 10** A photograph taken by Isaac Erb in 1918, showing the interior of a schooner under construction in Saint John. The keel and frames are clearly visible, as are the transverse beams (above). The ceiling has been started next to the keel.

Unfortunately, just after the frames were in place during construction of *Marco Polo*, Smith's luck ran out. A violent winter gale ravaged his yard, and the frames and other freshly built components of the ship's skeleton fell apart and scattered widely. Though the damage was quickly repaired, some have speculated that the frames were not replaced in the correct order after the storm and that the incorrect placement somehow contributed to the ship's unusually fast speed. It seems unlikely, however, that master shipwrights like Smith and Fredrickson would have made structural errors of that magnitude.

After the frames were retrieved, replaced, and bolted to the keel, the crew turned its attention to the interior of the vessel. The keelson, a strong piece of wood running the full length of the ship, was fixed firmly in place over the keel. Further timbers, called sister and rider keelsons, were inserted to add longitudinal strength. Planks were then placed lengthwise and fastened to cover the inner surface of the frames up to the lowest level of the ship's three decks. This layer, termed the ceiling, added further rigidity to the overall structure and prevented damage to the frames from the cargo. Next, thick transverse beams of pitch-pine were installed to add crosswise strength and carry the flooring for each of the three decks. At about this time, the hatchways were framed and placed to ensure good ventilation, and the sleeping quarters for the captain, mates and crew were completed. Stout wooden knees were installed to fasten the transverse beams securely to the frames. Then, the bow ports of the timber carrier were cut and finished.

Next, the outer skin of planking was fastened to the entire external surface of the frames with black iron spikes and treenails. This was a time-consuming and skilled job which required the best from even highly experienced crews. Each plank had to be curved to the exact shape required for its lengthwise position on the hull, often after a period in the steam-box to render it more pliable. The planks, cut to shape in the sawpit, then had to be planed and bevelled to ensure an exact and snug fit in all three dimensions. This was done by eye without involved mathematical computations.

The planking on the outer surface of the hull and decks of *Marco Polo* was then ready for caulking, the last major job prior to painting. Caulking, a repetitive and monotonous task, involved filling the seams between the planks with hemp fibres (called oakum) and hot tar. This process bound the planks closely to each other, making the hull nearly watertight. The oakum was forced into the seams first with caulking irons, then with mallets specially designed to make a pleasing musical note when struck, in an attempt to make more appealing an otherwise unpleasant job. The caulking process was completed with the application of a layer of hot tar using mops. After cooling and hardening, the excess tar was scraped off, leaving a smooth, watertight surface, ready for the application of paint.

*Marco Polo* and its contemporaries in the Maritimes were stoutly built for insurance purposes and, of course, to withstand the fury of ocean storms. The keels of these large, square-rigged vessels measured twenty inches by fourteen inches in cross section, and the keelsons were formed by eight timbers, each fourteen inches square. Planks for the ceiling ranged from five to nine inches in thickness, and those fastened to form the outer layer of the hull were five to eight inches thick, depending on where they were located. The transverse beams, knees, and other interior components were equally massive, giving the ships enormous internal strength, but encroaching greatly on their cargo-carrying capacity. Despite this, it was not uncommon in the nineteenth century for one of these wooden vessels to break up and sink in a gale, often with the loss of all on board. The ships did carry open boats on deck that could be used as lifeboats, but these were hardly equal to the full force of waves in an angry sea.

For construction materials, as much tamarack as could be found was used because of its lightness, durability and strength, but black birch, American white and live oak, pitch pine, white pine, black spruce as well as maple, white cedar and white elm all had their uses.

When the hull of *Marco Polo* was nearing completion, its rudder was built and hung from its sternpost; more specialized fittings, such as windlasses, capstans, binnacles, steering gear, and pumps, were also installed. Each of its three wooden masts (an iron mast was installed later) was built up from selected spars thirty-five to forty feet in length. Where needed, each mast was encircled tightly by iron bands for added strength. Subsequently, each mast was lowered through close-fitting, aligned apertures in the decks, and securely anchored into a slot in the keelson. Almost certainly, the ship's yards, manila rope rigging, and sails were installed while it was still on the stocks. That way, after being launched into Marsh Creek, the ship could be taken immediately down

**Figure 11** Ships under construction at Courtenay Bay near East Saint John, circa 1860.

**Figure 12** The original carving of a reclining Marco Polo taken from the ship's stern. The carving is now in the collection of the New Brunswick Museum in Saint John, New Brunswick.

to Courtenay Bay fully rigged and ready to handle the high tides in the Bay of Fundy. *Marco Polo* could then be loaded dockside with timber at Saint John, and sent on its way to Liverpool.

While almost all of its rigging was standard for the period, *Marco Polo* was equipped with Henry Cunningham's roller reefing system, a complex arrangement of ropes, iron blocks, chains, and rollers that rotated the yard as it was lowered, and wrapped the sail around it. This innovative feature permitted *Marco Polo's* topsails to be reefed from the deck, rather than by hands aloft laying-out on the yards. This saved time and effort, and provided an important safety feature for the crew in heavy weather. Whether or not *Marco Polo* was "salted" (the tempering of a ship's timbers with brine to prevent rot) has not been recorded. The disadvantage to salting was that the salt could leach out and contaminate the ship's cargoes.

When completed in April 1851, after a construction period of about eighteen months, *Marco Polo* weighed 1,625 tons and its keel measured 185 feet in length (a few more than its rival, *Beejapore*). Its beam amidships was thirty-five feet and the depth of its hold twenty-nine feet. It had three decks, eight feet apart, three masts, and was square-rigged. Its upper deck had small shelters at each hatch, but otherwise it was flush and uncluttered. Its colourful figurehead, fastened to its bow below its bowsprit, was a life-sized carving of Marco Polo, confidently leading the ship to fame and fortune. On its stern were other carvings of Marco Polo, one of him in western dress and another showing the famous traveller reclining and enjoying a well-earned rest. Also on *Marco Polo's* stern were carvings of an elephant and a star—perhaps intended to evoke images of the original Marco Polo atop an elephant and following his star, in the land of Kublai Khan.

## A DISASTROUS LAUNCH

As an aid to launching *Marco Polo*, James Smith's crew had constructed a wooden slipway, leading from under the vessel deep into Marsh Creek. A wooden cradle was built and placed directly under the ship in position to take its full weight. Long, thick, wooden runners were attached to the bottom of the cradle and a thick coat of grease was applied to the full length of the slipway and under the runners. Chains and ropes held the vessel in check as it was gradually wedged and jacked off its keel blocks onto the cradle. With all its weight on the cradle, the restraints were released, and, with an enthusiastic cheer from the crowd, the ship moved on its runners down the slipway into Marsh Creek. It was high tide and the date was April 17, 1851. The *New Brunswick Courier* from April 19 describes what happened next:

> We regret to learn that after this fine vessel had got clear
> of her ways in launching, she touched the bank of the creek,
> and the wind blowing fresh at the time, went over on her
> beam ends, in consequence of which some of the persons
> on board were hurt. One boy saved himself by jumping
> overboard and swimming ashore. The vessel, we understand,
> was not injured.

True, the ship was not damaged, but there it was, over on one side and stuck in the mud of Marsh Creek. While it was lying there, the uneven pressure from the weight of the ship on the keel caused it to become curved so that it was six inches higher in its middle than at its ends. This abnormality, called "hogging," was a common problem for wooden sailing ships after they had been in service for a considerable time. For a ship to begin its career hogged was quite unusual. It has been suggested that the upward distortion of the keel in its mid-section gave *Marco Polo* its legendary speed.

Smith's crew raced against time to right the ship and dig and haul it out of the mud before any further damage could occur. Fortunately, they were successful, and about two weeks after the original launching the ship was re-floated in Marsh Creek.

The full-sized ship has been described in detail by Michael Stammers in *The Passage Makers* as follows:

> The Marco Polo was sharp in her entrance with a flaring
> bow, straight floors, rounded bilge, a good run aft, with a
> straight keel and a straight sheer. Except for her draught (29
> feet depth of hold) she had all the characteristics of a New
> York packet, but was built larger. Thus her hull shape plus
> her size made her potentially a flier, and her deep draught
> meant that she could be driven hard too.

It is apparent, then, that the general design of *Marco Polo* was not novel. Rather, it was the combination of its large size in comparison to the New York packets, plus its shape, that made it seem so. Frederick Wallace, author of *Wooden Ships and Iron Men*, explains the features that together created this unique ship:

> *The Marco Polo was not a clipper in the true sense of the
> term, but she was of sharper model under water than
> the usual craft built at Saint John, and was regarded as a
> distinct departure from the common run of ships before her.
> Above the water, she was lofty and somewhat box-like—a
> great roomy, heavily-timbered vessel designed to pack a huge
> cargo and yet sail well. The true clipper was too sharp to
> carry much cargo, but in Marco Polo James Smith combined
> carrying capacity with an under-water body of sharp
> entrance and clean run—the true hollow bows of the clipper
> model being embodied—but amidships she had the bilge of
> the cargo-carrier.*

The revolutionary design prompted no small amount of argument and discussion, and some thought the ship would be a "dud." And while many observers, as documented by Elbridge White of Winnipeg, Manitoba, considered *Marco Polo* "a freak," and "as ugly as sin," they agreed that this complete departure in ship design held the promise of unmatchable speed.

*Marco Polo*'s "birth certificate" was entered in the Saint John Shipping Register on May 26, 1851. As recorded by Frederick William Wallace, it reads, "Ship *Marco Polo*, 1625 61/100 tons. Three decks and a half-poop. Length: 184.1 ft. Breath amidships: 36.3 ft. Depth of hold amidships: 29.4 ft. Standing bowsprit. Square-sterned. No galleries. Owned by James Smith and James Thomas Smith."

On May 31, 1851, being repaired and outfitted for sea, *Marco Polo* departed for Liverpool on its maiden voyage carrying a cargo of high-quality New Brunswick timber and some scrap iron. Captained by William Thomas of Saint John, who was just twenty-seven, it arrived in Liverpool in only fifteen days, a very fast crossing for the time. *Marco Polo*'s remarkable, record-breaking career on the high seas was underway.

# THE BLACK BALL LINE

## PURCHASE AND TRANSFORMATION OF *MARCO POLO*

*M*arco Polo arrived in Liverpool from Saint John on June 15, 1851, after completing its first trans-oceanic voyage in record-setting time. James Smith immediately offered it for sale, probably signalled to all by the presence of a broom tied to its mainmast, according to tradition. Unfortunately, it had arrived about three months too soon to catch the first wave of emigrants on their way to the goldfields of Australia, and the market for ships its size was otherwise sluggish. Also, some prospective purchasers may have been discouraged by its deep draft, which prevented it from entering the Liverpool docks except at very high tides; at all other times it would have to be loaded and unloaded using lighters. Whatever the reasons, the ship did not sell and was sent in ballast by Smith to Mobile, Alabama, to pick up a cargo of cotton. In Mobile, Captain Amos Crosby, another "Bluenose" from Yarmouth, Nova Scotia, took over the ship from William Thomas, and brought it back to Liverpool in thirty-five days during the fall of 1851. Amos Crosby is warmly remembered by Maritimers for saving the crew and passengers of the barque *Edisto* off the US coast in 1863. President Abraham Lincoln presented a gold pocket watch to him in recognition of this courageous rescue. The watch is part of the Yarmouth County Museum collection.

In February 1852, James Smith transferred all of the ship's shares to his son, James Thomas Smith, and travelled to Liverpool himself to see if he could sell the vessel. This time he was successful. It is likely that the first buyer was the colourful, well-known Paddy McGee, a Liverpool marine store dealer, fertilizer-works owner, shipbroker and co-manager of a line of Australian packets. Having acquired the ship at a good price, McGee then flipped it at a fine profit to another dealer-trader on the docks named James Baines. Baines had seen the ship at the Queen's Dock and had likely shrewdly concluded that it would be a flier because of its clipper-like lines below the water-line, and its massive structure, which would allow it to maintain its canvas in high winds, long after most other packet ships. No doubt Baines and his associates also conducted a thorough assessment of *Marco Polo's* carrying capacity and profit potential before purchasing it.

In due course, James Baines and his partners, Thomas Miller Mackay and William C. Miller, became the principal owners of *Marco Polo*. Together they had set up the Black Ball Line of packet ships to serve the wool trade and the rapidly growing number of emigrants headed for Australia, in competition with the other ship lines already on this

**Figure 13** This early stylized portrait of *Marco Polo* depicts it with full sails and flags flying. An unusually large ship, it must have been a magnificent sight on the high seas when running full out. This view of the ship was painted for its second captain, Amos Crosby, probably during his command in 1851.

run. "Black Ball" was an unfortunate choice for a name because two other Black Ball Lines were already in service, one between New York and Liverpool and the other between Saint John and Liverpool. In *The Passage Makers,* Michael Stammers speculates that the adoption of the Black Ball name by the Baines group was a "direct theft," designed to give the new firm instant public recognition at the expense of the other companies. Whether true or not, the name stuck, and in due course Baines's Black Ball Line became world famous. This was thanks in no small measure to the exploits of *Marco Polo.*

After being purchased by James Baines, *Marco Polo* was put into dry-dock, likely at the firm of Black Ball partners Miller and Mackay. There, it was extensively refit, transformed from a timber carrier into a top-notch passenger liner destined for service in tropical waters. During this make-over, in addition to extensive work on its passenger quarters, the original iron fittings were replaced with copper ones. As well, the hull was coated with a layer of felt and tar, then sheathed completely with sheets of copper to prevent fouling by marine animal and plant growths.

*Marco Polo*'s refitters were especially worried about a voracious marine organism called the Toredo worm, infamous for making large, disastrous burrows into the hulls of wooden ships. *Toredo navalis,* a mollusc shaped like an elongated clam, ingests wood particles that it obtains by boring into wood with two serrated shells ideal for making short work of hull planking. After much trial and error, ship builders discovered that copper was the best material to prevent Toredo worm damage. Easily worked to the shape of the hull, copper develops a surface scale over time that comes off along with whatever marine growth is attached to it; also, it does not rust and provides an impenetrable barrier to the Toredo. As an added bonus, copper sheathing, thanks to its property of exfoliation, is effective against seaweed and barnacles. Although barnacles do not attack wood, an accumulation of barnacles and seaweed can greatly reduce the speed of a vessel by increasing the drag on its hull. For these reasons, sheathing with copper became standard practice in the nineteenth century for the hulls of wooden ships that would be venturing into tropical, Toredo-infested, waters.

Following its metamorphosis, *Marco Polo* was returned to the docks in Liverpool and prepared and provisioned for its first voyage to Melbourne, with the soon-to-be-famous James Nicol "Bully" Forbes as its captain. A reporter for *The Illustrated London News* from February 19, 1853, provides a description of the ship as it appeared at that time:

> *When the tide of emigration from this country first set in towards the Gold Regions of Australia it experienced a great check, i.e. the length and tedium of the voyage. The ships which had previously been engaged in the trade to Australia were generally better calculated for carrying cargo than for speed, or the capability of affording comfortable accommodation for passengers; whilst from 100 to 120 days were actually consumed on the voyage out. An improved class of vessels very soon appeared, which, it was confidently predicted, would reduce the voyage to eighty days. A few clippers even promised greater things; and, from the beauty*

**Figure 14** The first drawing of *Marco Polo* to be published in *The Illustrated London News*, on February 19, 1853. The ship is close to its anchorage with its fore course, main course, and mizzen royal sails reefed. Almost all of its flags have been raised to signal its various affiliations.

*of their models and the perfection of their equipments, the promise appeared by no means unlikely to be realised. Still it was contended that a necessary amount of reliable speed for the voyage out and home could not be secured without the addition of steam-power.*

*In the meantime, however, a noble British ship—the* Marco Polo—*had already sailed from the Mersey, and was destined to achieve a triumph over both sailing-vessels and steamers greater than had ever before been considered possible by nautical men. The* Marco Polo *sailed from Liverpool, with a complement of passengers, on the 4th of July, for Port Phillip, and made the voyage out in the unprecedentedly short space of sixty-eight days! and the passage home in seventy-four days! Allowing for twenty-eight days spent in unloading and loading at Port Phillip, only five months and twenty-one days elapsed from her leaving and regaining the shores of Great Britain.*

*On the 10th of August, the* Marco Polo *was in lat. 32 west, bound for Port Phillip by the Cape of Good Hope; and on the 11th of November she was again in lat. 32 west, on her return by Cape Horn, having thus sailed round the world in two months and eight days.*

*The distinguishing feature of the* Marco Polo *is the peculiarity of her hull. Her lines fore and aft are beautifully fine, her bearings are brought well down to the bilge; thus, while she makes amidships a displacement that will prevent unnecessary 'careening,' she has an entrance as sharp as a steam-boat's, and a run as clean as can be conceived. Below the draught-line her bows are hollow: but aloft, she swells out handsomely, which gives ample space on the topgallant forecastle; in fact, with a bottom like a yacht, she has aloft all the appearance of a frigate.*

*The* Marco Polo *is a three-decker, and having been built expressly for the passenger trade, is nothing short in capacity or equipment. Her height between decks is eight feet, and no pains have been spared in her construction to secure thorough ventilation. In strength she could not be well excelled; her timbering is enormous; her deck*

*beams arc huge bulks of pitch pine; her timbers are well
formed and ponderous. The stem and stern frame are of
the choicest material. The hanging and lodging knees are
all natural crooks, and are fitted to the greatest nicety. The
exterior planking and ceiling is narrow; and while there
has been no lack of timber, there has been a profusion of
labour.*

*The length of the* Marco Polo *from stem to stern
(inside measurement) is 185 feet; but over all she will
make considerably more. Her beam is 38 feet, and her
depth of hold from the "coombings" 30 feet. Her register
tonnage is 1625, but her burthen will considerably exceed
2000 tons. On deck, forward of the poop, which is used
as the ladies' cabin, is a "home on deck," to be used as a
dining saloon; it is ceiled with maple, and the pilasters are
paneled with richly-ornamented and silvered glass; coins of
various countries being a novel feature of the decorations.
Between each pilaster is a circular aperture, about six feet
in circumference, for light and ventilation; over it is placed
a sheet of plate-glass, with a cleverly-painted picturesque
view in the centre, with a framework of foliage and scroll, in
opaque colours and gold.*

*The whole panels are brought out slightly by a rim of
perforate zinc, so that not only does the light from the
ventilator diffuse itself over the whole, but air is freely
admitted. The saloon doors are paneled with stained glass,
bearing figures of Commerce and Industry, from designs
by Mr. Frank Howard. In the centre of the saloon is a table
or dumb-waiter made of thick plate glass—which has the
advantage of giving light to the dormitories on the deck below.
The upholstery is in embossed crimson velvet.*

## THE DISCOVERY OF GOLD IN AUSTRALIA

Meanwhile, in the Southern Hemisphere, a momentous event was
underway, one that would determine much of *Marco Polo's* future. The
great Australian gold rush began in 1851 and brought hundreds of thousands of people to southeastern Australia. *Marco Polo* was refitted in

time to meet the huge demand that arose in the fall of 1851 for ships to transport prospective miners from Britain to Australia. The men were anxious to reach Australia before the rich alluvial gold deposits were worked out, and *Marco Polo*, with its size and speed, was ideal. The ship, like a successful miner, had struck gold.

The first discovery of gold in Australia, and the subsequent gold rush, began, oddly enough, in California. In January 1848, James Marshall discovered gold on the American River in the tail-race of a sawmill he was building for John Sutter. News of the discovery travelled fast, setting off a huge influx of miners into San Francisco from near and far, especially the east coast of the United States, the British Isles, and Australia. Australia, in particular, went California-mad and experienced an exodus of young men.

Among those venturing from Australia to San Francisco in 1849 was a former stockman named Edward Hammond Hargraves, aged thirty-three. Hargraves, a large man, had worked on ships as a cabin boy, on sheep and cattle stations, and as an innkeeper. On July 17, 1849, after leaving his wife with five children and the inn, he shipped out on *Elizabeth Archer* bound for San Francisco to seek his fortune. He remained in California for over a year but, like so many others, was unsuccessful in his quest for gold. He had arrived too late and the big fortunes had already been made from the rich, easily worked, alluvial deposits. But Hargraves was a quick, astute learner and gained much knowledge about placer mining during his brief stay at the California diggings. In particular, he learned how to separate gold particles from surface dirt by swirling an iron pan and rocking a specialized wooden box called a cradle. He also became adept at recognizing geological features that heralded the presence of gold. Most important of all, he realized that the features that characterized the gold-bearing Sierra Nevada region of California were also present in New South Wales, Australia, in the plains just west of the Blue Mountains. Then and there, Hargraves decided to return to Sydney, travel across the Blue Mountains, and seek gold among the same kind of hills, gullies, and rocks that he had worked in California. It was several months before he could obtain passage, first to Hawaii and then back to Sydney on the schooner *Emma*. His patience paid off, however, for Hargraves's revelation was the idea that led to the first great Australian gold rush.

On January 7, 1851, Hargraves arrived in Sydney to resume his quest for gold. Upon his return, he re-entered a colony in serious trouble; many businesses, including the family's inn, were faltering. With Australia losing men by the score to the gold fields of California, there was an urgent need to reverse the stampede quickly before the entire economy collapsed. For his part, Hargraves realized that he held the solution in the palm of his hand—if he could just discover a payable gold deposit.

On February 5, 1851, Hargraves headed west to the plains around the town of Bathurst. There, at the Wellington Inn, he met a fellow prospector named John Hardman Australia Lister; the two set off to explore a nearby creek and river. They only found a few specks of gold, but that was enough for Hargraves to exclaim to Lister, "This is a memorable day in the history of New South Wales. I shall be a baronet, you will be knighted, and my old horse will be stuffed, put in a glass case, and sent to the British Museum."

Hargraves and Lister teamed up with some friends of Lister, two brothers named William and James Tom, and Hargraves showed them all how to build a rocking cradle to extract gold. The four of them then prospected for gold along nearby Lewis Ponds Creek. They worked together for a week, but without success. Hargraves then left to visit his wife while the other three continued the search, this time along another nearby waterway called Summer Hill Creek. On April 7, 1851, the three prospectors struck gold, this time in a "payable" amount (i.e., an amount sufficient to provide a return for their efforts). As previously agreed, they informed Hargraves of the strike and gave him the small bag of gold they had collected. The prospectors named the gold-bearing area Ophir, after a well-known gold mining camp Hargraves had visited in California, itself a Biblical allusion to King Solomon's gold.

Hargraves was a natural publicist and knew exactly what to do next. On May 6, 1851, he announced the find in a fired-up, self-congratulatory speech in Bathurst. This resulted in a frenzied stampede to the site of the find, as reported in the *Bathurst Free Press*. Hargraves approached the Colonial Secretary, Mr. E. Deas Thompson, claimed all the credit for himself and petitioned for his reward. His reports neglected to mention the important role of his three collaborators. The partners later took legal action and eventually received recognition and retribution. After verification of the find by the colonial government's

geologist, Hargraves received most of the credit and was rewarded by
the New South Wales government and the government of neighbour-
ing Victoria. He was named Crown Commissioner for Exploration of
the Goldfields and, in 1854, travelled to England and was presented to
Queen Victoria.

The discovery of ample gold at Ophir became one of the most
important events in the history of Australia. Reported in the *Sydney
Morning Herald* on May 15, 1851, the discovery was officially
announced on May 22 by Governor Fitzroy, who simply stated that
gold had been found in commercial quantities near Bathurst. Ships
carrying passengers, mail, and newspapers from Australia brought
this momentous news to Britain and America about three months
later. On September 2, 1851, news of the gold strike was reported in
the British newspaper *The Times* and, in the same month, gold from
Australia arrived for the first time in England aboard the ship *Thomas
Arbuthnot*. A letter by its master, G. H. Heaton, describing the chaotic
scene in Sydney was printed in *The Times* a few days after the ship's
arrival. By the end of the year, thanks to such publicity, demand for

PORTRAIT OF MR HARGREAVES, THE DISCOVERER OF GOLD IN AUSTRALIA—[FROM A
PHOTOGRAPH BY FRITH]—see page 4.

**Figure 15** A drawing
of Edward Hargraves
(also Hargreaves), gold
prospector, 1864.

passage to Australia skyrocketed and packet-ship owners were scrambling for space. By the beginning of 1852, forty thousand men were busy extracting gold at the "diggings."

In all, about 70 million British pounds worth of gold were mined in New South Wales. As well, new and important strikes soon followed the Ophir discovery, at Ballarat and Bendigo Creek, north of Melbourne, and in other parts of the country. Immense quantities of gold were recovered, and from 1851 to 1860 Australia accounted for 39 per cent of the world's gold production, compared to 41 per cent for the United States.

To produce the gold, large numbers of miners and their families came to Australia during the gold rush years, giving an enormous boost to the local economy and the shipping lines serving the colony. As well, men abruptly left their jobs and joined in a furious rush to the goldfields from all corners of Australia. Ships were left without crews, shops without clerks, fields without farmers, and ranches without stockmen. Basil Lubbock, in his 1921 book, *The Colonial Clippers*, describes the "diggers" and the tumultuous, colourful scene in Melbourne:

> *Lucky diggers, down on the spree, easily distinguishable*
> *by their plaid or chequered jumpers, cabbage tree hats,*
> *moleskin trousers, and bearded, swarthy faces were to be*
> *seen everywhere. Many of them spent their time driving*
> *about in gaily decorated carriages accompanied by flashily*
> *dressed women covered with cheap jewellery. Amongst*
> *these charioteers, the uproarious British tar could always*
> *be picked out. He disliked driving at a slower pace than a*
> *gallop, and as often as not, instead of handling the ribbons,*
> *he would insist on riding postillion—and he was also*
> *unhappy unless his craft flew a huge Union Jack.*

Among the diggers was young Charles Napier, a prospector in the Kingower Fields. After a time, he wrote his younger brother Sam, encouraging him to leave the family home in Bathurst, New Brunswick, and join him in the search for gold. Sam, who was only twenty, must have had an adventurous streak: Without hesitation, he decided to follow his brother's advice, and in 1857 signed up as a crew member on board a ship bound for Australia, *Marco Polo*. Soon after the ship completed the voyage and docked in Melbourne, Sam joined Charles in the goldfields. Luck must have been on their side—on August 27, 1857, they struck gold in the form of a gigantic nugget weighing 1,743.13 ounces, as well as two pounds of quartz clay and iron oxide. Measuring 2'4" x 18" x 10", the nugget may have been the largest one uncovered in the world to that time. It was named the Blanche Barkly, after the daughter of Governor Barkly of Victoria. Unsurprisingly, the Napier brothers became famous after their discovery, and immensely rich after selling the gold to the Bank of England. Like Hargraves, they too were granted an audience with Queen Victoria; a replica of their nugget (the original was broken up) was placed in the British Museum. Charles returned to Australia and Sam to New Brunswick. In New Brunswick Sam served as a politician in the 1870s before falling on hard times. He died in 1902, in an isolated cabin in the Ottawa Valley while working for a logging company.

The role that *Marco Polo* and its sister ships played in the great Australian gold rushes was enormous. The only way prospective miners and other emigrants could travel to far-off Australia was by undertaking a long and perilous sea voyage, and the packet ships offered the best opportunity for a rapid and successful passage. Hundreds of thousands travelled that way and the famous *Marco Polo*, year after year, was one of the prime carriers. In all, *Marco Polo* made about twenty-five round-trip voyages with the Black Ball Line between Liverpool and Melbourne from 1852 until 1867, and carried about fifteen thousand immigrants to the new land. In a very real sense, these wind- and steam-driven ships, such as *Marco Polo*, gave the colony its future.

## THE REMARKABLE MEN OF THE BLACK BALL LINE

During its years of operation, from 1852 to 1871, the Black Ball Line was a "Jewel in the Crown" of Queen Victoria and the British Merchant Marine. Ships like *Marco Polo* and the four beautiful clippers built by Donald McKay of Boston became world famous in their own time, and their fame has endured. During its peak years, the Black Ball Line was a large firm. For example, in 1860 it purchased or chartered close to eighty-five wooden sailing ships built chiefly in Canadian or American yards and employed about three hundred officers and three thousand seamen. These large ships served mainly on the Australian service, transporting manufactured products, specie (coins), many tens of thousands of emigrants to Australia, and valuable exports of wool and gold back to England. Such trade was so crucial to the new colony's future that the Black Ball Line, together with its competitors, fundamentally changed that part of the world.

Three men, all now legends in the annals of the British merchant marine, played the chief roles in the story of the Black Ball Line. Each brought a very different set of skills to the enterprise but all three were aggressive, clever and bold, and they complemented each other perfectly. They were the colourful James Baines, shipbroker and entrepreneur; the solid and reputable Thomas Miller Mackay, shipbuilder and manager; and the quick-tempered James Nicol Forbes, ship's captain. Although there were several other owners and many Black Ball captains, these three were the leaders and the ones that gave the line its special character. The three were not interested in running just another shipping line—and they worked long and hard to improve their ships in every possible way. Intent on achieving true excellence with a fleet of large and fast wind-driven ships, they become the envy of the maritime world. Their success lasted for almost twenty years.

James Baines, one of the most famous shipowners and brokers in the history of the British merchant marine, was born in Liverpool in 1823, into a family in the sugar and confectionery business. His father died when he was only five, leaving his mother with three young boys and a girl to bring up. Fortunately, she succeeded and, in addition to running an excellent boarding house and a sugar refinery, became an accomplished and well-known pastry chef, complete with an appointment to Her Royal Highness, the future Queen Victoria.

According to Michael Stammers, Baines probably went to a lower-class trade school to learn practical subjects rather than a school for future gentlemen, emphasizing classical Greek and Latin. After a brief and unhappy sojourn as an apprentice to a local engineer in a grimy machine shop, Baines began work in the 1830s as a shipping clerk with his uncle, Richard Baines, a shipbroker. This was the start of his long and illustrious career in the shipping business.

As a clerk, Baines learned how to charter vessels and arrange contracts between shipowners and shippers with cargo to transport, as well as being involved in ship insurance deals, ship construction contracts, and the day-to-day activities of the office. As a young man, Baines was energetic and hard-working. Over time, he gained a deep appreciation of all aspects of maritime commerce. He recognized that this was a business that required little capital at the start and would favour a sharp deal maker with a persuasive personality. Baines possessed the latter two qualities in abundance and badly needed a profession that would allow him to get in at the bottom without much in the way of resources. By all accounts, Baines displayed a charming and generous personality as he grew older, but he could also be a sharp businessman—tough, uncompromising, and even callous and devious when necessary. Such qualities were definitely an asset in the rough-and-tumble of the Liverpool waterfront.

In appearance, James Baines was a short man by today's standards, about five feet and three or four inches tall, with reddish hair. He typically dressed as if he aspired to be an English gentleman, in a frock coat and a bow tie. Michael Stammers in *The Passage Makers* described him as follows:

> *a handsome face with a firm chin and strongly modelled mouth and nose, with kindly eyes, all fringed by the fashionable 'mutton-chop' whiskers and a mop of thick curly hair. His clothes are of the latest cut. The high collar and stock, with its jewelled pin, suggests there is something of the dandy about him. The heavy pouches under the eyes hint of burning the candle at both ends.*

Baines lived with his mother until he married Anne Browne of Netherton, in 1848, when he was twenty-five. They had a son and three daughters, and, once Baines was established, lived a prosperous existence in big houses with lavish furnishings and many servants in a good part of Liverpool. Baines was a remarkably enthusiastic, generous, and charming man who loved to promote his business at big banquets on his ships and at smaller dinner parties at home.

Baines' business career had many ups and downs although, overall, it was remarkably successful. He began in 1845, working with John Hamilton and then Joseph Carter in the shipping business as a shipowner and charterer. He quickly became involved in a variety of complex financial transactions, since his pattern was to leverage his investments heavily with large loans from the bank and investors. He was on his way towards becoming a financier as well as a shipping magnate and began to work closely with Israel Barned, Charles Mozley, and other directors of Barned's Bank. This alliance remained crucial to Baines and the Black Ball Line until, overextended, Barned's Bank collapsed in 1866.

In 1849, Baines started his firm, James Baines & Co., going into business on his own as both a shipbroker and sugar refiner. He then purchased his first Canadian-built ships, mostly of medium size, from Nova Scotia and Quebec. In the process, he came to appreciate the high quality of many Canadian shipyards and their products. Also at that time, he developed a working relationship with Captain James Nicol

**Figure 16** A statuette of James Baines now located in the Merseyside Maritime Museum.

Forbes, master of *Cleopatra*, a ship partly owned by Baines. Then, in 1851, the shipbuilder Thomas Miller Mackay joined Baines' firm, completing the promising threesome.

Baincs & Co. established the Black Ball Line in 1852 principally to take advantage of the huge demand for passage to the gold fields of Australia. The firm quickly bought *Marco Polo*, and Baines boldly ordered a quartet of large and graceful vessels from Donald McKay's yard in East Boston for delivery between 1852 and 1855. *Lightning*, an extreme clipper, was the first of this group. The others, in order of acquisition, were *Champion of the Seas, James Baines*, and *Donald McKay*. These clippers were true wonders of the sailing world—beautiful to look at and expertly and soundly built, each one unique. James Baines' huge gamble in purchasing these American vessels paid off handsomely. The grouping of *Marco Polo* with the McKay quartet in the Black Ball fleet gave James Baines, Thomas Mackay, and "Bully" Forbes an unbeatable combination.

Donald McKay (no known relation to Thomas Mackay) was born in Shelburne, Nova Scotia, in 1810, into a farming family. His father was a British Army officer who had moved to Nova Scotia after service during the American revolutionary war. When he was quite young, McKay moved to the United States and apprenticed with the famous shipwright Isaac Webb of New York. He then went on to become one of America's leading ship designers and builders. Since they were contemporaries, working a short distance from each other, it seems likely that James Smith and Donald McKay kept in close touch, visited back and forth, and traded ideas and possibly even designs.

Early on, there were a great many competitors to James Baines' Black Ball Line on the Australian run, but the two most notable ones were Pilkington and Wilson's White Star Line, and Gibbs, Bright & Company's Eagle Line. The latter were owners of the huge Brunel-designed ship, *Great Britain*, powered by steam as well as sail, which became one of *Marco Polo's* chief competitors. Other smaller lines such as the Golden Line, the Thistle Line, a short-lived Temperance Line, and even a White Ball Line also competed for a time on the Australian run.

During the 1850s, Baines and the Black Ball Line flourished, thanks in no small measure to a string of successful voyages to Australia by

*Marco Polo* and the McKay-built clippers. However, in April, 1858, Baines' fortune changed abruptly. The beautiful Black Ball liner *James Baines* was consumed by fire while at berth at the Huskisson Dock in Liverpool. Fortunately, the loss was covered by insurance, but nonetheless, Baines and the Black Ball Line had suffered an immense blow. Further, competition from the White Star Line was increasing. In order to counter that threat, Baines was forced to partner with Gibbs Bright & Co. in 1858 in an effort to offer an improved service to Australia. Throughout all of this, however, Baines was buoyed by an outpouring of sympathy from the citizens of Liverpool on the loss of the magnificent clipper named after him. At this time in his career he was very popular and held in high esteem by almost all.

Despite the setbacks, Baines and his partners continued to work diligently to improve and enlarge the Black Ball fleet through a series of acquisitions. In 1862, twenty-seven ships were purchased; in 1863, another twenty-three were acquired, and several others were chartered. Baines and his partners also attempted to establish a steamship service to Australia through a series of stock allotments that took advantage of new British legislation. The entire stock manipulation scheme collapsed, and much of the blame rightly fell on Baines' shoulders. His favourable reputation as a businessman took a decided turn for the worse; he was even lampooned in the Liverpool press as "Jerry Bunce" and "Jamie Bubble."

Baines' ill fortune continued. In January 1866, the fine Black Ball clipper, *Hannah More* (also built by *Marco Polo's* James Smith), was completely shattered in a hurricane off Lundy Island near Bristol, with the loss of nineteen crew members. Then on May 1 of the same year, with the shipping industry in a steep downturn, Barned's Bank, deeply in debt, failed completely. Barned's Bank had been the chief financial support for the Black Ball Line, and Baines and Mackay quickly found their company to be more than half a million pounds in debt. The liquidators moved in immediately and forced the two owners to sell more than two thirds of their fleet of more than sixty vessels. *Marco Polo* ended its passenger service with the Black Ball Line in 1867 when it failed to pass the passenger survey and was put into cargo service. In 1871, it was sold to Wilson and Blain of South Shields, to transport coal and timber. Somehow, through the financial wreckage, Baines and Mackay managed to keep the Black Ball Line afloat. Baines' wealthy brother-in-law, John Morris, invested heavily in the line, other Liverpool shipowners chartered vessels to them, and several money-saving alterations were made, including dissolution of the partnership with Gibbs, Bright & Company. Hence, the Black Ball Line regained some prominence during 1869–70, but nothing like its former glory. Then in April 1871, the line failed completely and the partners went their separate ways. Baines, not to be denied, set himself up in business the way he had started, as a shipowner and shipbroker.

Shortly after the collapse of Barned's Bank and the Black Ball Line, Baines received another huge blow with the death of his wife in 1872. Nevertheless, he soldiered on as a shipbroker, shipowner and marine insurance agent. His business acumen remained as sharp as ever and he continued to be consulted often by members of the Liverpool business community, always giving of his advice willingly and without restraint. On March 8, Baines died of liver cirrhosis and heart failure, at age sixty-six. In *Fast Passage To Australia*, David Hollett notes that Baines died at 24 Nile Street, "a humble, but respectable address" in Liverpool. He was buried in Smithdown Road Cemetery, not far from his old friend, the master of *Marco Polo*, James Nicol Forbes. His obituary in the *Liverpool Citizen* ended in this fashion:

> *In the pages of our local annals, and in the history of navigation, the name of James Baines will always stand in the foremost rank as having been one of the greatest leaders of his time.*

Thomas Miller Mackay, the son of a soldier, arrived in Liverpool as a young man from his native Scotland in 1831. Little is recorded about him until 1849 when he began a long and successful career as a shipbuilder in partnership with William Cowley Miller. The solid and reputable firm of Mackay and Miller first built ships but then switched to ship repair and refitting when a flood of relatively cheap, large, and sturdy wooden vessels reached the Liverpool market from North America during the 1850s. In the mid-1850s, the firm turned to the production of large iron vessels, anticipating the switch from wood to iron as the preferred shipbuilding medium that would take place during the latter half of the century.

Mackay's partnership with James Baines and the Black Ball Line began in 1851 and became a productive and profitable union for both men for almost twenty years. Baines was adept at purchasing and chartering ships, setting up companies and arranging financing, while Mackay, the shipbuilder, knew ships inside and out. He could tell Baines the true value of a ship, present and future, and he also knew what could be done to upgrade a vessel so it would be of increased value to the line. Further, the shipyard he ran with Miller on the Mersey stood ready to actually carry out needed repairs or even refit an entire ship if needed, without delay.

Mackay contributed to the Black Ball Line in a variety of other ways. He was an excellent manager and he handled many of the business affairs of the line. This likely included scheduling voyages and dock space and ensuring that ships had adequate provisions and first-rate captains and crews. Caring for the never-ending needs of the passengers would have kept him busy too. Mackay also handled much of the company's interface with the local authorities, including the Mersey Docks and Harbour Board, of which he was a member. He also handled what we now call public relations, and in his role as spokesperson for the company, he sent a steady stream of letters to *The Times* that promoted the interests of the Black Ball Line and kept its name in the public eye. He even had the distinct honour of welcoming Queen Victoria on behalf of the company when she toured two of its ships, *James Baines* and *Champion of the Seas*, while they were docked at Portsmouth waiting to load troops on their way to quell the Indian Mutiny. By all accounts, Queen Victoria was surprised and pleased by the quality and carrying capacity of these vessels.

Little is known of the private life of Thomas Mackay. Stammers records that he had a son and a daughter, and that his son became a partner in his business in 1867. Mackay was well connected and well thought of in the Liverpool business community, and had a number of distinguished friends including the famous archaeologist and member of Parliament, Austen Layard.

When the sailings of the Black Ball Line ceased in 1871, Mackay's brilliant partnership with James Baines came to an end. The magnificent and exciting Black Ball years ended as the graceful wooden packets were gradually replaced by steam-driven, iron-hulled vessels. Mackay switched into the phosphate business as a manager, though he probably remained active as a shipbroker as well. He continued in those capacities until his death, close to the end of the century.

James Nicol "Bully" Forbes, the notorious Black Ball captain, became a legend in his own time. Probably the most colourful and famous of all the great British merchant marine captains, Forbes was known for his hair-trigger temper, his boastfulness, and his abusive attitude toward his crew and even his passengers. Once he allegedly levelled a pair of loaded double-barrelled pistols at his crew to force them to keep all sails set in a gale. In an address to his passengers at the start of his second voyage on *Marco Polo*, he is said to have boasted, "Ladies and Gentlemen, last trip I astonished the world with the sailing of this ship. This trip, I intend to astonish God Almighty!" No one can say that Forbes lacked confidence! He was also very athletic; it is said he thought nothing of climbing out onto the end of a boom to survey his ship as it raced along before the wind.

Yet there was another, more positive side to Forbes, who was sometimes underestimated in the sensationalist articles written about him. In addition to being bold and utterly fearless, Forbes was a highly-trained, well-rounded master mariner who could accurately size up the sailing capabilities of a vessel in an instant. He knew how to take advantage of the positive qualities of a ship, and how to get the most out of his crew, even if his methods were sometimes crude and even belligerent. Also, he was well ahead of his time as a navigator. He knew thoroughly the essentials of great circle sailing and Maury's charts, so the routes he plotted for his ships consistently took full advantage of the curvature of the earth and the prevailing winds and currents. His skill at navigation was so good that his ships kept within five miles of their plotted course for days on end. No wonder Forbes' ships, throughout his entire career, recorded remarkably fast passages and achieved one speed record after another.

Forbes was born in Aberdeen in 1821 into a distinguished Scottish family. Like James Baines, he was fairly short by today's standards, only five feet, seven inches in height, and had reddish hair. He studied navigation and other naval subjects in preparation for a career at sea and apprenticed aboard an Aberdeen ship when only twelve. In 1839, he moved from Scotland to Liverpool and began his meteoric career as a sea captain working on ships trading between Canada and Britain. Very soon after his arrival, he was made master of one vessel after another and he gained attention quickly because the ships he commanded consistently made unusually fast passages, even those that were not built for speed.

Forbes's big break came in 1851 when James Baines noticed the bold, highly aggressive, and successful way he approached his job. As a result, in 1852, when Forbes was only thirty-one years old, Baines gave him the demanding position of captain of the newly refurbished *Marco Polo* bound for Melbourne. As noted earlier, to everyone's utter astonishment, Forbes and *Marco Polo* made the voyage around the world, to Melbourne and back to Liverpool, in five months and twenty-one days, a world record. Almost immediately, *Marco Polo*, Forbes, Baines, Mackay, and the Black Ball Line became famous throughout the maritime world.

As a reward for his success, Baines gave Forbes command of *Marco Polo* for a second voyage to Melbourne in 1853. This time the ship made it out in seventy-six days and back to the Mersey in ninety-five days with some very fast daily times. Next, Baines placed Forbes in command of the new, especially speedy, Black Ball clipper *Lightning*, just built for the line in the McKay yard in East Boston. Forbes and *Lightning* were a potent combination too, and the ship made it from Liverpool to Melbourne in seventy-six days, and back to Liverpool in the record time of sixty-four days. Forbes' boast for the voyage, "Melbourne or Hell in sixty days," had almost come true.

"Bully" Forbes was now at the pinnacle of his career and was more than ready for his next assignment. At that time, James Baines had just purchased another magnificent clipper for the Australian run, *Schomberg*, from its builder, Alexander Hall of Aberdeen. Based on Forbes' outstanding record, Baines asked him to be the first captain of this brand new and unique Scottish-built vessel and Forbes jumped at the chance. Unfortunately, this would turn out to be an ill-fated decision that would plague Forbes for the rest of his life.

*Schomberg*, named after Charles F. Schomberg, head of the Liverpool emigration service, was one of the finest large clipper ships ever built. Designed to resemble in shape the large and successful North American clippers, it was remarkably well constructed with frames of stout English oak and several layers of thick planking of larch and pine placed diagonally to each other. Its first class accommodation was easily as lavish as *Marco Polo*'s and included a smoking room, a library, a ladies' saloon, and a grand piano. Well ventilated and comfortable, *Schomberg* was the Scottish answer to the challenge of the large wooden North American clippers, and it carried a great deal of Scottish pride every mile of the way.

With this huge responsibility resting on his shoulders, Forbes, in command of *Schomberg*, proudly left Liverpool on October 6, 1855, bound for Melbourne. Also on board were 481 passengers, their life possessions, 115 crew members and three thousand tons of heavy railway equipment. A banner boasting, "Sixty Days To Melbourne" proudly flew from the ship's halyards. The passage to Australia was largely uneventful, although frustratingly slow by Forbes' standards. The ship sailed without its main-topmast for four days in October and did not meet consistently strong trade winds until in sight of the coast of South America. Once given strong winds, it proved its speed by making one run of 368 miles in twenty-four hours. It finally reached its landfall in Australia at Cape Bridgewater, west of Melbourne, on December 25.

On the evening of December 27, the ship was tacking in towards shore and breakers were clearly visible. Some accounts place Forbes below at this time playing whist while the ship moved closer to land. Forbes was alerted by the Mate, came up on deck, and ordered the ship about, but the attempt was unsuccessful as the ship was caught in a strong, uncharted current. He then tried to wear the ship to by bringing it stern to windward, again without success. *Schomberg* then went aground on an uncharted sandspit about thirty miles west of Cape Otway. Forbes and his crew tried valiantly to free the ship, but it was hard aground in four fathoms of water. The next day, all passengers were safely transferred in an orderly manner to the steamer *Queen* and transported to Melbourne without further incident. Over the next few days, a moderately successful effort was made to salvage as much of the ship's cargo and luggage as possible. Then, the once beautiful clipper, now at the mercy of the sea, broke up completely, taking with it Scotland's high hopes for glory and Forbes' high standing among captains in Britain's Merchant Marine. Fortunately, the ship and its cargo were fully insured.

Subsequently, at a formal inquiry, Forbes was absolved of all blame for the disaster. Both the current and the sandspit that had destroyed the vessel were uncharted, and the jury foreman concluded that Forbes had used all necessary precautions to try to save his ship. However, at a special meeting called to discuss the wreck, many of the passengers who had lost all their possessions severely censured Forbes, calling him "tyrannical and grossly immoral," and no doubt many other names as well. These charges became widely known.

Following the wreck of *Schomberg*, Forbes' formerly good reputation was irretrievably tarnished despite vigorous efforts to salvage his name. He was able to retain enough of his standing to allow him to continue for a time in his career as a ship's captain. He carried on his record of fast passages, and may have taken *Marco Polo* for one final voyage in the 1860s.

In his personal life, it is known that Forbes was married in 1853, but his wife was unwell and died just eleven years later. They had only one child, a daughter who married and had two sons. After his last voyage, Forbes retired to a house overlooking the Mersey in the district of Everton and died at age fifty-two, on June 4, 1874. On his tombstone in Smithdown Road Cemetery is the simple inscription: "Master Of The Famous Marco Polo."

# LEAVING HOME FOREVER

## LIVERPOOL AND PREPARATIONS FOR DEPARTURE

*D*uring the nineteenth century, and especially during the century's middle decades, Liverpool became the major gateway for emigrants departing the British Isles for the overseas settler colonies. A great many ships—driven by sail, steam, or both—were pressed into service to transport these passengers. As one might expect, some were fast, well-built, clean, and sanitary, while others were just the opposite: unsafe, filthy, and infested with vermin and deadly infectious diseases. In 1852 *Marco Polo* took its place in this great transoceanic movement of passengers, acquitting itself admirably. In fact, in due course it became one of the best of the packet ships and a champion among all emigrant ships traversing the oceans of the world. The surprising success of this ship from Canada that started life as a humble lumber carrier is a fascinating story.

To ensure the financial success of the first voyage of *Marco Polo* in June 1852, James Baines chartered the steerage accommodation on the ship to the Government Emigration Commissioners, and agreed to crowd about 750 destitute emigrants bound for Melbourne onto its three decks. This group, mainly from Scotland, included single men and women, married couples, and 327 children and infants. The impoverished emigrants had little to lose. Like the refugees from the Irish potato famine who had crowded into Liverpool on their way to North America in the 1840s, this group, in the 1850s, also had endured lives of hunger, disease, and abject poverty in conditions almost unimaginable today. They came to Liverpool because of its good railway links, and because most emigrant ships like *Marco Polo* were based there. The adults were ready to work hard to make a good life for themselves in Australia, but no doubt all were well aware that with some luck, quick profits could be made from mining. They wanted to get to the Australian gold fields as quickly as possible before the fields were depleted.

Many emigrants were forced to spend a considerable period of time in Liverpool while their ship was made ready to sail and they arranged their departures. To these people with little or nothing in the way of funds, Liverpool could be a hell on earth offering vile, overcrowded, pest-ridden rooming houses, raging epidemics, thieves, swindlers , or "crimps," and precious little to eat. The "crimps," trading on the naivety of the emigrants, attempted to gain their confidence and then fleece them in every way possible. The future steerage passengers made out as best they could in their lodging-houses. But even so, some fell victim to one or more of the many contagious diseases endemic in the city, dying before ever boarding ship. Others, unknowingly, incubated infectious diseases and carried them from their pitiful lodging-houses onto ships like *Marco Polo*.

In *Passage to the New World*, David Hollett describes the lodgings then in use for emigrants passing through Liverpool:

> *The lodging-houses were little more than filthy overcrowded slums, into which as many as a hundred emigrants would be crammed, despite the fact that most of these dens were only licensed to cater for a fraction of that number. Men, women, and children would be bedded down together, and often on a cold stone floor, without any blankets. Here the emigrants would be robbed, cheated, overcharged, and run the very considerable risk of contracting a variety of contagious diseases. This deplorable state of affairs eventually led to the establishment of well-regulated Emigrants' Homes...*

It is true that conditions did gradually improve, but, hugely overcrowded and without adequate sewers and a clean water supply, central Liverpool remained an ideal repository in the mid-nineteenth century for contagious diseases of all kinds. Epidemics of cholera, typhoid fever, typhus, diphtheria, tuberculosis, scarlet fever, whooping cough, measles, and venereal and other diseases recurred with depressing regularity. The statistics are telling. In Liverpool in 1849, 5,245 died from cholera, 1,271 from diarrhoea and dysentery, 567 from typhus,

419 from measles, 376 from whooping cough, and 317 from the strep-
tococcal infection known as scarlet fever. Even when epidemics were
absent, these and other contagious illnesses remained prevalent in the
community, a major threat to all passengers intent on embarking from
the port by ship.

Of course, not all of *Marco Polo*'s passengers were penniless and
forced to travel in steerage. There were a select few who were wealthy
enough to afford fine hotels, first-rate meals, and cabin-class accommodation on board ship. These individuals had experiences that were
quite different from those of their steerage travelling companions. Freed
from the daily necessity of finding a place to sleep and food for their
families, they could explore the delights of the city while their servants
arranged their passage and packed their boxes. They had the time and
money to visit Liverpool's shops, museums, and botanical gardens, as
well as its major buildings such as the Town Hall, the Custom House,
and the huge new St. George's Hall.

Sarah A. Wilkinson was one such fortunate. She was an Australian
cabin-class passenger on *Marco Polo* on its largely uneventful voyage
from Melbourne to Liverpool from April 19 to August 3, 1862. Like a
number of her cabin-class companions, she kept a travel diary and in it
she describes outings to Liverpool's tourist spots such as the botanical
gardens:

> We left [the museum] with intentions of going to Botanical
> Gardens. After walking more than a mile we were told we
> had not got more than 1/2 way so entered an omnibus which
> took us to the park gates. The grass is indeed beautiful &
> such a bright green. It is like treading on a carpet of rich
> velvet. This is the 1st day I have yet seen & have admitted
> we have nothing to equal it in our country. The park is laid
> out very prettily with walks, seats and trees, from there
> we entered the gardens. They have a very peculiar way of
> making the beds of many shapes, curves, rings, diamonds &
> in one place an immense bird all made with bright flowers
> & shaped out by the grass carpet around them. We went
> through the hot houses, immense ponds bananas, ferns,
> aloes & pines…

In the following days, before returning to Australia, Sarah Wilkinson continued her European tour, visiting London and Paris and staying in first-class hotels. From her account, it is obvious that in the mid-nineteenth century Liverpool could be a delightful place to visit for a member of the leisure class.

## THE DÉJEUNER ON THE POOP DECK

On July 1, 1852, just two days before the departure of *Marco Polo*, a luncheon in celebration of the ship (called a "déjeuner" by the news-papers of the time) was held under an awning on the ship's poop deck. Banquets like this were commonly held by the major shipping firms in Liverpool to mark vessel departures and to gain publicity, since the banquet speeches were regularly reported verbatim in the newspapers. About eighty notables, including members of the local and national press, attended the gathering on *Marco Polo*. In general, they felt the ship was a large step forward in luxury and size compared to its prede-cessors. The assemblage heard in turn from all the key people involved with the ship, including James Baines, Thomas Mackay, Captain Forbes, and James Smith, its builder, who was visiting Liverpool from New Brunswick at the time. James Baines spoke first, and his words, as recorded in the newspapers of the day, reflected the optimism of the shipowners following the start of the Australian gold rush:

> *I rise with great diffidence to give you my best thanks for*
> *having this day honoured myself and co-owners of the*
> *Marco Polo with your company, and I may perhaps be*
> *excused in feeling some degree of pride in being one of the*
> *principal owners of this, the largest vessel and carrying*
> *the greatest number of passengers, ever chartered by the*
> *Government or despatched to Australia with passengers.*
> *That we shall endeavour to carry out our contracts with the*
> *Commissioners with satisfaction to them and the passengers*
> *and with credit to ourselves, I think I need not say, in which*
> *I am sure we shall be aided to the greatest extent by my*
> *friend Captain Forbes and all the officers of the ship, and*
> *I am much mistaken if the Marco Polo does not earn for*
> *herself such a reputation for speed that when on her return*

*she takes her place as one of the Black Ball Line, she will
receive for herself a bumper [i.e., a toast].*

A Mr. Munn of the Cunard Company followed Baines. His company
had been started in 1839 by Samuel Cunard, a native of Nova Scotia.
He noted that *Marco Polo* was the largest passenger ship to be sent to
Australia to date, and, accordingly, stood the best chance of becoming
the most prosperous. After Munn, Thomas Mackay spoke of the heavy
responsibility he felt for the welfare of the nearly one thousand people
who would be on board the ship. He emphasized the trust he had in
Captain Forbes and the ship's two doctors. James Smith, not surprisingly, spoke highly of the quality of Canadian-built ships and warned
of the dangers of unbridled American competition. Finally, Captain
Forbes was given his opportunity to speak. This was the moment everyone had been waiting for, and Forbes did not disappoint. He remarked,
referring to *Marco Polo*, that he judged from the appearance of the
ship's "sticks and timbers that she would be obliged to go" and that they
"must not be surprised if they found *Marco Polo* in the River Mersey
that day six months." This comment, although entirely in character for
Forbes, was both boastful and audacious since no ship in history, sail
or steam, had made the round trip passage to Melbourne and back
nearly as quickly as that.

## FORBES, MAURY, TOWSON, AND GREAT CIRCLE SAILING

Was Forbes merely showing off when he made that remark or did he
know something the others did not? In fact, there is evidence that
Forbes had such an advantage, as he was in possession of an entirely
new navigational approach largely unknown to the members of his
audience and the general public. Forbes had been in touch with John
Towson, an examiner in navigation with the Liverpool Marine Board.
Towson was an advocate of a new method of route selection that he
called composite sailing, a modification of great circle sailing. Great
circle sailing, known to mathematicians before the time of Columbus,
determines the best course to follow between two ports by taking
advantage of the curvature of the earth; composite sailing adds consideration of the prevailing winds and currents and navigational hazards.
Composite sailing was possible because Lieutenant Matthew Fontaine

Maury of the US Navy had carefully documented, and recently published, the prevailing winds and currents worldwide for different times
of the year. Maury had devoted his working life to the study of winds
and currents, with input from sea captains all over the world.

Forbes must have listened attentively while Towson (likely using
a globe as well as a flat Mercator chart) explained to him the advantages of following the earth's curvature by using a great circle route
to Melbourne and back, even though this would mean reaching deep
southern latitudes, especially the icy and dangerous "roaring forties" and
"howling fifties." Towson and Forbes likely calculated that *Marco Polo*,
by following a great circle route, could reduce the time and length of the
return passage by about 20 per cent over the old Admiralty route, which
had long been in use. Also, the Admiralty route to Australia took ships
close to the Cape of Good Hope, and many of them spent time re-pro-
visioning in Cape Town. In contrast, anxious to establish a new world
record for the Black Ball Line, Forbes would take *Marco Polo* directly to
Melbourne and back, without stopping on either leg of the trip.

Thus Forbes did have an important ace up his sleeve when he made
his celebrated boast at the Black Ball banquet. In time, Forbes turned
out to be the first of many Black Ball ship commanders to follow
Towson's recommendations, and *Marco Polo* became the first of the
Black Ball fleet to successfully follow the new great circle route from
Liverpool to Melbourne and back. Towson's principles, though, had
been successfully tested earlier when, in 1850, a Captain Godfrey followed a great circle route and successfully guided the 578-ton barque
*Constance* from Plymouth to Adelaide in a record-setting seventy-six
days. *Constance* left Plymouth on July 17, 1850, and arrived at Port
Adelaide on October 1 of the same year, creating quite a stir.

## INTRODUCING THE CREW

On its maiden voyage to Australia, *Marco Polo* carried a crew of thirty
regular able seamen and thirty others who were working to earn their
passage to the gold fields. Only a few days before the ship was sched-
uled to sail, the crew was selected by Forbes' mates from the large pool
of experienced seamen carousing in lodgings and alehouses near the
Liverpool docks. "Crimps" regularly assisted in this by plying some of
the men with liquor and then kidnapping those too drunk to resist.

These men, originally from both Western Europe and North America, likely would have been attracted to *Marco Polo* in any case because it was headed to the gold mines of Australia. Later, they must have been very pleased to see how large and well-built this new ship was and how nicely it was fitted out. In fact, it was the largest and most modern pure sailing ship in the port.

**Figure 17** The interior of a typical female emigrants' home.

**Figure 18** This detailed drawing shows a crowd of rather apprehensive passengers embarking on an emigrant ship in 1880.

While mostly superstitious and illiterate, the members of the crew were quite proficient at their jobs, although they have been described as a rough and ready lot, drinking and brawling whenever they got the chance. Most had benefited from several years of experience on the high seas, even though the average age was only about twenty-five. The crew included members of many different trades. For example, in 1854, on *Marco Polo*'s third voyage from Liverpool to Melbourne, the ship's newspaper (*The Marco Polo Chronicle*—see Appendix) listed the following: six cooks, two bakers, one butcher, fourteen stewards, two stewardesses, twelve musicians, a bosun (boatswain) and a bosun's mate, two carpenters, a sail maker, thirty-four seamen, and five boys. The captain and his four mates ruled the ship with an iron fist, but the two surgeons on board had considerable influence too, especially over matters directly affecting health such as cleanliness and sanitation. In due course, with practice, the officers and able seamen formed a superb team, adept at handling the rigging and sails in even the most difficult and dangerous conditions.

It was customary in those days to place a miniature farmyard on board large sailing ships so that fresh meat, fowl, and eggs could be provided for the captain and his cabin-class passengers throughout the voyage. The selection of animals brought on board was surprisingly large; in the case of *Marco Polo* it usually included four hundred chickens and rabbits, ducks, geese, thirty pigs, thirty sheep, and a few cows. Passengers viewing this menagerie must have felt they were on board a veritable Noah's Ark. Probably some of *Marco Polo*'s crew members spent a good deal of time trying to figure out how they could partake of this source of fresh food without being discovered.

## BOARDING THE SHIP

While James Baines and the others were enjoying their "déjeuner" on *Marco Polo*, the ship's passengers and crew were making arrangements to board the vessel. For the steerage passengers in particular, this process was both emotionally trying and physically exhausting. A long and sometimes terrifying voyage lay ahead of them. Almost all were leaving Britain permanently with no prospect that they would ever return, even for a visit. Very likely, they would never see their relatives and friends again, or visit the familiar surroundings where they had lived their entire lives. Their job prospects in Australia were uncertain, and the world they were about to enter both on board ship and in Melbourne was completely unknown to them. Even the letters they would write in the future to Britain from Australia would take three or more months to reach their destination, if they arrived at all. As well, because of this uncertainty, letters were likely to cross in the mail, making a continuous correspondence almost impossible.

For many passengers, this voyage would become the most important event in their lives and a true turning point from a life of misery to one with some promise. Of course, many of these indigent steerage passengers couldn't have appreciated that at the time, and it's no wonder many of them approached the trip with a good deal of trepidation and dread. An excerpt from *The Illustrated London News* of April 13, 1844, sums up the situation of the departing passengers admirably:

> *There is, perhaps, something extremely melancholy at the idea of quitting our native land—perhaps forever; the ties of kindred, the bonds of locality, cling round the heart, and true it is that absence only serves to strengthen the links that unite us to HOME; for in whatever part of the world an Englishman may be, he still looks with ardent affection and longing desire to the spot of his nativity. But with all these feelings, dear and precious as they are—on second consideration, there is not so much to excite painful sensations in emigration as first there seems to be. A large field is opened for skill and industry; there is a prospect of gaining a competency which promises a "welcome return"; and unhappily there exists in England so much real distress, that anything in the shape of improving the condition must be grateful to the feelings. It is true the voyage is long, and no one who understands the nature of the fickle elements but must be sensible of the many unpleasantnesses attendant upon a tedious passage in a crowded ship; but when these are overcome, and there is health and strength, and a willingness to labour, they are soon forgotten in the quiet of occupation on shore.*

But before boarding the ship, the emigrant passengers had preparations to conclude to keep their minds off the uncertainties that lay ahead. Even though the steerage accommodation on board *Marco Polo* had been chartered by the British emigration commissioners and the emigrants' fares were paid in full or in part, the passengers still needed to check in at the busy and sometimes chaotic Black Ball office at 6 Cook Street near the Mersey River. There they received their "Passenger's Contract Ticket" and registered and labelled what luggage

**Figure 19** Passengers saying farewell to their loved ones, probably forever, 1887.

they possessed for eventual placement in the ship's hold. The ticket was a true contract and receipt that listed the name of the ship, the class of accommodation and meals, and a pledge by the line to provide the transport paid for.

The emigrants also received a list of items essential for the trip, which could be purchased in shops nearby, either singly or in kits put together especially for them. Those passengers and families needing financial assistance to acquire these items sometimes were aided by small grants from the emigration commissioners. The emigrants were expected to provide their own bedding, eating utensils, soap and toilet articles, drinking mugs, cans for water, and wash basins. Warm clothing, appropriate for the voyage, was also recommended, and clothing articles to be purchased were listed in some detail. Those who could, bought a stock of preserved food to take along. As well, craftsmen were encouraged to bring the tools of their trade. For steerage passengers, only one box of possessions could be carried on the ship and kept in the berth; all other boxes and chests had to be clearly marked for the hold and delivered to the luggage depot on the dock designated by the Black Ball Line. Only cabin-class passengers could bring furniture on board.

The placement of luggage on board the ship could turn into a day of excitement and adventure, as it did for William Culshaw Greenhalgh. In his log, written in the spring of 1853, Greenhalgh described the multiple difficulties he encountered in placing his luggage on board *Marco Polo*:

> *I got my luggage on board, had great difficulty in getting it measured, which prevented me procureing a porter in time before the Ship left the Basin, she left me standing along side of my luggage, as if I was to be left. Hired a Donkey Cart to take the luggage to Princess Pier, had great trouble with the porters, had engaged them previous…for [one shilling] and [they now] desired [eleven shillings]. I was not to be imposed upon and tendered them their [one shilling].*
>
> *Off I went with the Donkey Cart well loded a distance of 1 mile had not traveled far, when a friend Harry that was with me discovered one of the wheels coming off. He cried out "whoa" seised the wheel I flies to the Donkey's head, fortunately he was not bad to stop, or we should have had an upset, we examined the wheel & found a piece of bone*

*as a substitute for the lin nale of course we had to repair*
*the wheel, had got nothing that whould act, but found by*
*looking about in the street an old can, we twisted the wire*
*that was round the top, & made it fit very well, got Mr.*
*Donkey on his journey once more, my friend watching the*
*wheel I holding the boxes, the Boy coaxing the Donkey, had*
*a great row with the boy, he proved like the rest an imposter,*
*charged [five shillings] we paid him [one shilling] & gave*
*him a few coppers to hold his noise, were informed that the*
*tug was not going to the Ship any more, of course in another*
*fix, hired a ferry boat for [ten shillings] Harry & a friend*
*went with the luggage to get it on board arrived along side*
*the Ship, the tide being very high, caused the rope to slip, &*
*was washed down the river a distance of 6 or 7 miles, were*
*expected to be upset the boatman was a complete blaguard,*
*struck them both several times & threatened to pitch them*
*overboard, got the luggage back quiet safe but with great*
*difficulty, charged [ten shillings, six pence] for running the*
*risk of loosing it altogether, the tug left for the Ship at 4PM,*
*arrived on board all right, met with my Bro. Jim & Mrs*
*was busy arrainging our Births, returned with the tug to*
*Liverpool, spent a pleasant evening together.*

Such was a day in the life of William Culshaw Greenhalgh, who was a passenger on *Marco Polo* on its second voyage from Liverpool to Melbourne in the spring of 1853. Passengers on all voyages of the ship may well have experienced similar difficulties.

A few days prior to boarding the ship, the steerage-class emigrants were moved from their vile billets in Liverpool's lodging houses to the emigrant depot, which had opened in 1852 at Birkenhead, across the Mersey from Liverpool and the Black Ball office. In this strictly regulated depot, an old warehouse, the single men were separated from the single women and the families placed in between. All were closely crowded into one large room on the first floor; fortunately, the room was dimly lit or there would have been little privacy. The beds were apparently almost rock hard, but the meals, served in a mess room on the ground floor, were adequate and probably better than any the emigrants had eaten for quite some time.

The accommodations at the depot were not unlike those the emigrants would encounter on board *Marco Polo*, so, in a sense, the depot provided a transition between the relative freedom of life on shore and the strict confinement of life at sea. Nevertheless, one can imagine the shock among the emigrants when faced for the first time with the reality of living for months in such crowded quarters with no possibility of escape. Unfortunately, the close crowding of the emigrants at the Birkenhead depot and on board the ship would provide an ideal breeding ground for the spread of communicable diseases, especially among the infants and children.

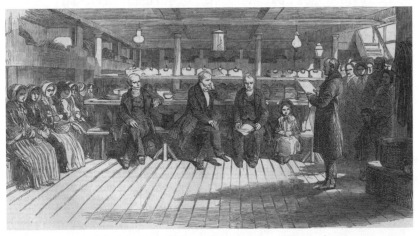

**Figure 20** Female emigrants being given advice prior to departure.

**Figure 21** Passengers enjoying a meal.

While the steerage passengers crowded into the Birkenhead depot, the cabin- and intermediate-class passengers were allowed to remain in their comfortable hotel rooms until just before the ship sailed. Then, once all the steerage passengers had been installed in their billets on the ship, these first- and second-class passengers, well-dressed for the occasion, boarded at their leisure. The all-powerful Captain Forbes followed. *Marco Polo* was usually anchored in the Mersey during the loading of both passengers and cargo since the draft of this large ship was too great, and the ship berths too shallow, to allow it to be stationed dock-side except at very high tide. Accordingly, lighters had to be used to load the ship's cargo while a steam tender ferried the passengers from the Pier Head, a floating landing stage. The lack of dockside berths deep enough for large ships like *Marco Polo* was a continuing problem for the Black Ball Line and one that Thomas Mackay debated regularly with the port authorities.

Mrs. William Graham of Inneskillin, Ulster, an intermediate-class passenger in 1863, describes what was it like to board *Marco Polo* and spend a first night on the vessel:

> *Having embarked in the Marco Polo of the Black Ball*
> *Line upon the 5th August 1863 we found ourselves in the*
> *midst of such confusion with the crowds of passengers and*
> *luggage that we thought it morally impossible order could*
> *be restored or rather instituted for some time however piles*
> *of boxes became less as evening wore on with the crowds*
> *of passengers wandering through the ship inquiring for*
> *the number of their berths as if it were a town about ten*
> *o'clock quietness to some extent prevailed for the first time*
> *I mounted into my limited bunk destined to be my place of*
> *repose for many a night it was impossible to rest well the*
> *first night people taking the heat and the strangeness of the*
> *place prevented me from sleeping for some time when I did*
> *close my eyes I had a kind of broken slumber but indeed it*
> *was impossible to feel at ease in such quarters on the first*
> *night next morning the getting up was an effort the dressing*
> *operation having been performed partly on deck where*
> *we were required to go for water and to wash there also, it*
> *were useless to attempt description of the breakfast which*

*we managed to get after a good deal of delay owing to the*
*numbers going with all sorts of vessels to bring the black*
*tea which we must take or want certainly it was far from*
*inviting in its appearance and the flavor was worse.*
*Having gone on shore for some necessaries I got well*
*wet before returning to the ship which was about five in*
*the evening. I had some difficulty getting on shore the*
*Government officer having had the passengers pasing... in*
*review before him which is termed an inspection supposed to*
*be a very strict affair but really a sham.*

The health inspection Mrs. Graham refers to was, as she suggests, a quick affair since its main purpose was only to screen for active infectious diseases. Carried out by surgeons under the able direction of Captain Charles F. Schomberg and his small team of emigration officers, the inspections almost certainly would not have detected those in the incubation period of a potentially serious illness. To do so would have required taking a fairly detailed medical history from each passenger to determine if there was recent contact with anyone suffering from a communicable disease. Given the large number of passengers passing through Liverpool, the small complement of inspectors available, and the limited knowledge of disease transmission at the time, detecting major diseases was beyond the scope of the inspectors.

Schomberg and his team of about a dozen inspectors did gain an enviable reputation on the docks in Liverpool as they assiduously went about their job of determining if each passenger vessel had clean accommodations, sufficient edible food, clean water, and adequate light and ventilation. They had the power to confiscate any ship that did not meet their standards and the specifications of Britain's Passenger Acts. Captain Schomberg was so highly respected (or so open to flattery) that he had a ship named after him by James Baines and the Black Ball Line. Unfortunately, the ship was the same *Schomberg* that Captain Forbes eventually led to an untimely end on the coast of Australia.

## ACCOMMODATIONS

Once on the ship, the separation of the steerage passengers into single females, families, and single males was maintained strictly. The single men were given bunks forward, the single women aft, and the families were placed amidships, to separate them. Stout partitions divided the groups, although these probably had large openings to permit ventilation. Not an inch was wasted in the steerage compartment. The berths were about six feet square, and four to six people were accommodated in each one. Double bunks, placed one on top of the other, were standard, and the children were usually crowded below. Curtains for the bunks were provided but there was little privacy, as all dressing and undressing had to be done either on the bunks or in the limited space between them. Separate lavatories were provided for each sex, and long tables, benches, and chairs were placed in the centre of the room, where the cramped passengers could unwind and take their meals. Close to 750 steerage passengers were accommodated in this way on *Marco Polo*'s three decks during the ship's first voyage to Melbourne.

Don Charlwood, in *The Long Farewell*, describes the crowded scene in steerage:

> We can visualize every peg with its smocks and coats and headgear hanging from it; every shelf laden with such home foodstuffs as the passengers were able to bring; the wide table strewn with metal mugs and plates and cutlery; each bunk occupied by men, women and children, some sitting, some lying. Then we can imagine the whole in motion, rolling from side to side, timbers creaking loudly as seas rise, children falling and crying and seeking comfort from parents who want only to lie down or to vomit—and where is there to vomit? As seas rise higher, scuttles must be screwed down by the ship's carpenter, plunging the whole steerage into semi-darkness while utensils are dashed into the long passageways.

The small group of cabin-class passengers on *Marco Polo* was much better off. They had individual cabins about six feet square, located aft around the sides of the ship, and they had access to the poop deck for exercise, as well as the sumptuously appointed dining saloon. The cabin-class passengers fitted out their cabins with their own furniture, shelves, and adornments as they wished, and often employed one of the ship's carpenters to assist. Everything had to be firmly fixed in place to prevent accidents during rough weather. The doors of the cabins opened into a central corridor, which, in turn, led to the luxurious saloon where meals were taken.

James Cooper Stewart was a cabin-class passenger on *Marco Polo* when it left Liverpool under Captain James Clarke on June 7, 1857. A native of Brecklin, Forshire, Scotland, Stewart went on to become one of Australia's leading citizens. A successful lawyer, he was elected to Melbourne's city council in 1870 and served as the city's mayor in 1885–86. On completion of his voyage on *Marco Polo*, he wrote a letter to his father, dated September 27, 1857, describing his passage. Here is his account of his initial encounter with the ship:

> *Friday, 5th. I took my luggage to the pier, had it measured and put on board the steam-tug which was lying out in the river. You can scarcely realise my feelings when I felt myself leaving the shores of Great Britain, for I was really downcast but I put the best face upon matters that I could, and a feeling of confidence possessed me as we neared the noble ship. I was among the first to ascend the plank and spring on deck. A terrible bustle then ensued everyone running in his neighbours way upsetting porters with trunks etc. and many were the curses impreacted on our heads. I soon found out my berth and got everything I wanted out of my trunks, which were then stored away. My berth was a little room well lighted and ventilated about 6 ft. by 4 ft. and 8 ft high—all plain wood—and contained two bunks the one above the other. I chose the top one as it seemed to be the best, the lower one being only some 18 inches from the bottom of the top one while the latter was fully 3 ft. from the roof. Between the side of my berth and the bunks there is only about 2 1/2 ft. left for turning round and making your bed etc. Our Cabin or Saloon is very nicely fitted up—the seats are cushioned the tables are covered with waxcloth, and the windows are of stained glass in the centre of each being a picture of the principal towns in Australia. The Intermediate have no saloon or Cabin but must eat their meals either 'tween decks or on the main deck. The Steerage are the same. Six sleep in a berth in the Intermediate and Steerage. The Steerage*

*occupy the forepart of the vessel—the Intermediate—the*
*centre and the 2nd Cabin and Saloon Passengers the Aft or*
*Quarter deck.*

The captain also had a well-appointed cabin, and it is likely that the pursers and surgeons did too. These were aft, opening onto the central corridor or onto the spar deck. The ship's wheel and binnacle were placed at the rear of the poop, and the helmsman and officer of the watch could be found there. The other members of the crew were billeted in cramped quarters right in the bow of the ship, in the topgallant forecastle. Here, during their off-duty hours, they probably discussed endlessly the glittering possibilities about to be presented to them on their arrival in Melbourne, their city of gold.

As James Stewart noted, *Marco Polo* also accommodated a number of second-class or intermediate passengers. Members of this group were berthed, four to six to a bunk, in cramped private quarters located between decks. Their meals were truly of an intermediate standard—not as good as cabin class, but fully cooked and much better than the fare in steerage. Like those in cabin class, they had steward service, took their meals separately in crowded quarters and generally kept their distance from the emigrants in steerage. Not surprisingly, though, the intermediate passengers eagerly accepted invitations to move up in status and join the cabin-class passengers in leisure activities in the saloon or on the poop deck.

There was also separate accommodation on board packet ships for passengers who were extremely ill and pregnant women about to deliver. These hospital areas, typically one for men and one for women, contained only a small number of beds and did not offer the doctors much opportunity to isolate contagious patients.

In his report for 1852, the health officer for the colony of Victoria identified 888 passengers on *Marco Polo*'s first voyage from Liverpool to Australia. Of these, the best evidence suggests that 750 were emigrants in steerage and 138 were in cabin or intermediate class. Most of the latter did not consider themselves emigrants since, presumably, they had the resources to return to England if they wished. Over all, 327 passengers were children and 661 were Highland Scots. Adding the 60 crew members to the 888 passengers gives us a grand total of 948 "souls" (as they were called in the manifest) who placed their futures and, indeed, their very lives in the hands of Captain Forbes and the Black Ball Line.

## A Church Service Prior to Leaving

In a letter written to his father in September of 1857, James Stewart includes on account of a church service held his first day on the vessel, while it was still anchored in the Mersey. The service followed the usual perfunctory health inspection. Emotions were obviously running high as separation loomed:

> *The Government Inspector came on board at 11 o'clock and examined us all but the examination is all a mockery for he only asks "Are you quite well" and of course receives for his answer "yes." About 4 o'clock a Clergyman came on board and announced that public worship would be held on poop at six in the evening. Such an intimation was received and*

**Figure 22** An emigrant ship being towed out to sea by a steam-driven tug in 1844.

*responded to joyfully by the greater body of the passengers.*
*At the appointed hour the minister ascended the poop and*
*asked us to sing the 64ᵗʰ paraphrase it being done with*
*more than ordinary solemnity, he offered up a prayer for*
*our safety and welfare. He then delivered an address with*
*great fervour and eloquence touching beautifully upon our*
*separation with our friends and I need scarcely add that*
*the sobs which were distinctly audible and the tears that*
*trickled down the cheeks of the oldest and the youngest were*
*unmistakeable evidences of the sympathy and reception*
*which his remarks met with in the hearts of his audience.*
*With a doxology and blessing this interesting and impressive*
*ceremony ended.*

## THE DEPARTURE

*Marco Polo* departed on its first voyage from Liverpool to Melbourne
on July 4, 1852, with much cheering, waving of handkerchiefs, and
firing of the ship's cannon. It is probable that James Baines was on
board to bid the ship a fond goodbye as it proceeded down the Mersey,
after which he would have left the ship to return to Liverpool on a
tug. Although a first-hand account of the 1852 departure has not survived, there is a record of *Marco Polo*'s departure on its second voyage
to Australia in March of 1853. No doubt in their essentials both departures were similar, but by 1853 *Marco Polo* had become quite famous
and thousands were present to bid it goodbye.

Edwin Bird, like William Greenhalgh, was a passenger on *Marco
Polo* during its second voyage to Melbourne. In his diary, Bird leaves a
detailed record of the exciting scene that unfolded as the ship weighed
anchor and was towed by a steam-driven tug down the Mersey towards
the sea:

> *She hall'd out of the Salt House dock on Wednesday the 9th*
> *March 1853 at 1/2 past 10 O Clock in the Morning....*
> *Our first day of Sailing was Sunday the 13th. The Tug*
> *Took us not far over the Bar as the wind was Blowing nicely*
> *down the River. When the tug left we gave Her to more*
> *Cannons and as many Huzars as the Lungs of the M Polo*

*would permit. I slept on Board last night for the 1st time but not so comfortable as I could wish. We were all in confusion this day giving up our tickets and arranging the Births and so on. We found one stowaway just in time to send Him back with the Tug. Had he not the Capt (Forbes) Swore He would Have chucked Him over Board. I and my friend Gisborne workd very Hard all day arranging our Birth and at last got it very comfortable. A cup of Tea and a Hard Biscuit for Breakfast and no diner. It was Ketch who could all in such Bustle and confusion and the Band on Deck played all the liveliest Tunes they could think of.*

Once the ship was on the Irish Sea, the passengers encountered the pitching and rolling of ocean travel under sail for the first time. Almost all became seasick and many remained ill for several days. Here is James Stewart's graphic description of his personal encounter with this disorder and its debilitating effects:

*Monday, 8th June. I jumpt up in the morning in the full belief that I was not to be seasick but no sooner did my feet touch the ground or the floor than my cranium began to revolve and ere you could say Jack Robinson the whole of my yesterday's meal (by this time reduced to a lovely pulp) went bang up against the wall of my berth, which example my mate soon followed. It seemed as if everyone had been waiting for someone to lead the dance, for no sooner did I give the key note then off they set at a rattling pace. I soon popped into bed where I felt considerably at ease, but the Dr. came and pulled me out saying I would be better to remain on deck. I was dreadfully sick and vomited freely. The sea was rough and nasty rains were falling.*

Once underway, *Marco Polo* was in many respects a microcosm of a Victorian town. A complex interactive society, sharply divided along class lines, existed on the ship. But disease was always a threat for all passengers since infectious diseases knew no boundaries and could jump from steerage to intermediate to first class overnight. The physicians on the ship made strenuous efforts to prevent this by conducting daily inspections that emphasized cleanliness, frequent washing, and good ventilation. Yet, as we shall see, their efforts were not always successful.

The speed of the ship and the duration of the voyage were probably the most important determinants of the passengers' comfort and safety. A quick transit meant less danger from disease, epidemics, and inclement weather, as well as a shorter exposure to the uncomfortable conditions on the vessel. In other words, there were very tangible benefits to be won. Lives would be saved, passenger comfort greatly enhanced, and valuable cargoes delivered in record time. The entire Black Ball fleet would bask in reflected glory from *Marco Polo*.

~ℰ *Four* ℰ~

# LIFE AND DEATH ON
# THE AUSTRALIAN PASSAGE

## CAPTAINS AND CREWS

*M*arco Polo must have been a magnificent sight as it left the Mersey and entered the Irish Sea on its way to Australia. Longer than half a football field, with masts higher than an eleven-storey building and capable of carrying as much as 22,000 square feet of sail, it had a commanding presence which no doubt piqued the public's fascination. Outstanding in all respects, *Marco Polo* would soon earn the well-deserved nickname "Queen of the Seas" as its exploits became more and more widely known.

All the adults on board *Marco Polo* knew that they would have to rely solely on their own collective resources to survive the passage since they would be alone and out of touch with the rest of humanity except for occasional, unscheduled encounters with passing vessels. The ship's captain, crew, and passengers would have to handle all crucial matters by themselves, including accidents, contagious diseases, and damage to the ship from bad weather and collisions. In effect, the ship's departure meant that an entire large community, complete with all its

**Figure 23** *Marco Polo* size comparison.

requirements, prejudices, and class distinctions, would be on its own, separated from society for two or more months and with no guarantee of a safe return. It took a good deal of courage, a strong spirit of adventure, and, in some cases, a sense of desperation for the emigrants to embark under these conditions. Yet they all did it.

Of course, the most important person on board *Marco Polo* was the captain. He was the supreme commander and was ultimately responsible for the fate of everyone on the ship. He had to navigate the vessel safely to its destination, in record time if possible, and he had to forge the crew into a hard-working, cohesive unit. The maintenance of discipline among passengers and crew was also his responsibility, and he had to be prepared to act directly to enforce order. Most passengers and crew regarded the captain with considerable awe and respect while they were on the ship. They watched and sometimes even recorded his every move. Not surprisingly, they also paid strict attention to the punishments he handed out for on-board offences, which included theft, fighting, drunkenness, and general mayhem. Penalties ranged from confinement to quarters to many forms of physical ill treatment, such as shackling and withdrawal of food and water. As the ship's court of last resort, it was the captain's responsibility to maintain discipline and order on his ship at all times, since chaos and even mutiny could be the alternative.

A good captain knew every feature of his ship, including the intricacies of its design and structure and its sailing qualities and capabilities, especially in rough weather. As a master of many trades, he could speak knowledgeably with his officers and men about most aspects of their jobs, from the best ways to stow the cargo to the best ways to handle the wheel, rigging, and sails. With the obvious exception of "Bully" Forbes, who had an aura of brutality and ruthlessness about him, most of *Marco Polo*'s Black Ball captains were typically judicious and temperate disciplinarians. They knew that if they acted tyrannically their officers would be quick to follow their example, so generally they responded to instances of insubordination and rudeness among the crew in an even-handed and calm manner. All in all, *Marco Polo*'s captains were responsible for controlling a pretty rough group of men and overseeing a complex community. At the same time, they also had to navigate a sailing ship totally dependent on the wind for its forward motion on a predetermined course to a precise destination on the other side of the globe and back home again. The surprising thing is that all of them, including Forbes, did it so well that *Marco Polo* was able to make the Liverpool–Melbourne round trip many times with the regularity and consistency of a steam-powered ship and usually more quickly.

*Marco Polo*'s good luck with captains was largely due to the hiring protocols of the Black Ball Line: it was company policy to hire only experienced and accomplished mariners for the post, men who had outstanding credentials including the Master's Certificate of Competency. As noted, the colourful, quick-tempered James Nicol Forbes was the first to serve in this capacity from 1852–53. Forbes' former first officers on the ship, Charles McDonnell and R. W. (Edward) Wild, took over the post from 1853 to 1855. Next, from 1855 to 1863, came Captains James Clarke, D. H. Johnstone, and William Mitchell Arnold.

Aside from Forbes, the best remembered of this group is James Clarke. Like *Marco Polo*, Clarke (1823–94) was originally from Saint John, New Brunswick. He went to sea at an early age, advanced quickly, became chief mate of the barque *Liverpool* at only twenty years of age and obtained his first command of the small snow *Allegro* at age twenty-eight. Clarke was highly thought of by his fellow officers as smart and reliable, and as a good and sober seaman and scholar. Appointed a lieutenant in the British Royal Naval Reserve—like Captains Forbes and Arnold—Clarke became captain of *Marco Polo* in March of 1855 and sailed it with good success until December 1858. After that, he continued to work for the Black Ball Line as captain of *Lightning* until 1861. He retired in 1892 after fifty-five distinguished years at sea, and died two years later on the Isle of Man. He is fondly remembered today in New Brunswick as one of Canada's most outstanding mariners in the heydays of sail and steam.

While it was up to the captain to make the key decisions affecting the ship, it was up to his mates to see that they were carried out. This was not always an easy task, as crew members at that time could be tough, quarrelsome, and resentful of authority. The mates, for their part, could also be tough, sometimes shouting and even using brass knuckles on crew members who didn't do their jobs. But on the other hand, some of the mates spent many hours teaching the younger crew members and the apprentices the particulars of their profession.

To facilitate the work, the mates divided the crew equally into port and starboard watches and had the men work four hours on and four hours off, around the clock. The ship's bell signalled the intervals. The work itself was hard and dangerous. As the ship scudded ahead, the sails had to be furled and unfurled, the rigging adjusted, and the helm constantly attended to. In very rough weather, the seamen became drenched and had to hang tight to the yards and rigging for their very survival. Charlwood notes that in rough weather a man on a mast 150 feet above the deck could swing arc-wise for many yards on each side to the force of the waves. Then, after their shift was over, they had little choice but to retire to their narrow bunks in the topgallant forecastle which, as the most forward part of the ship, took the full force of the waves. No wonder it was not uncommon for crew members to be lost overboard during the course of a voyage. No wonder some sang to help pass the time as they performed repetitive tasks on deck. No wonder many of them spent their time in port in ale houses and in the beds of prostitutes until their money ran out and the "crimps" came, plied them with drink, and tricked them into signing on for another voyage.

On *Marco Polo*, most of the crew members, including the seamen, stewards, and tradesmen, were probably illiterate. Some were casual labour and not well trained, signed on only for the length of the voyage, but the able seamen knew their jobs well. They were constantly afflicted by a variety of illnesses ranging from venereal diseases to life-threatening acute infections, and most were broken in health by the time they were thirty or forty. Yet despite ill health, they shared a real pride in their ships and an appreciation of the power of the great oceans that surrounded them for most of their lives.

In his travel writing, W. D. Lawrence summarizes the many responsibilities of the captain and his crew members in these terms:

> *There has to be a constant watch kept to guard against danger and to watch the movements of the ship. The log, compass and the pumps have to be attended to. The chart has to be consulted and the lead kept ready at hand to obtain soundings. Observations of the sun and other heavenly bodies, by the quadrant, have to be taken every day if possible; and at 12 o'clock noon the time regulated, the courses steered marked down, the sight of the sun by chronometer time has to be taken and noted down, and all worked up to find the ship's position. In fine weather various*

*work is going on; some hands painting; others scraping the
spars, blocks and sometimes the dead-eyes; and some hands
making chafing gear, and various things too numerous
to mention. The captain or his officers watch every shift
of wind, and brace up or square the yards accordingly; at
one time hauling the bowlings and at another slacking off
the sheets; at one time sailing on the starboard tack, and
another on the port....*

*When a heavy gale comes, all hands are called to shorten,
reef or furl the sails, and if the gale is fair, and the ship
steers well, she is generally run before the wind, and it is a
beautiful sight to see a full-rigged ship scudding in a gale;
the rolling waves following her close up, and sometimes
dashing along her sides with all their raging fury.*

## The Passengers and Captains Speak

As we have seen, a number of passengers on *Marco Polo*, all probably
in cabin or intermediate class, have left us first-hand records of life and
death on the ship as it made its way around the world. These priceless
letters and diaries allow us to experience daily life vicariously on the
ship in good times and bad. They provide an immediacy that no second-hand description can equal.

The following letter, written by J. M. Whelan to his parents and
brother on October 4, 1852, is a superb example of such a record and
an extraordinary document in itself. Whelan was an upper-class passenger on *Marco Polo* during its first passage to Melbourne, and his
account vividly conveys many of the high and low points of that perilous and extremely uncomfortable voyage.

> *After many an adventurous scene, we have at last arrived at
> Melbourne and in good health.*
>
> *We sailed from the Mersey on 4th July in the ship Marco
> Polo [under] Captain Forbes.*
>
> *We had 960 souls on board and 70 crew, so you may
> guess that large as our ship was, it was pretty full. There
> were two surgeons on board, both Irishmen, of whom Dr.
> North was one of the finest fellows I ever met.*

*Nearly everyone on board, with the exception of about 20, were seasick more or less for the first week. I was one of the exceptions, having never had an hour's sickness from the time I went on board till I left. After the sea sickness had subsided, dysentery set in and Mary had an attack of it but owing to Dr. North's unremitting attention, it was soon checked.*

*Hugh Wallace and his wife had it, and Hugh's wife was very near going to Davy's locker [i.e., the bottom of the ocean] by it; after Mary recovered from this attack she got excellent health. We had no fever of any kind, but measles set in at the first and about 50 children, chiefly infants, died. Only two adults died on the passage and these were women who had been sickly coming on board, for the sea will in such cases either kill or cure.*

*From the time we sailed, the weather grew hotter every day until we came to the line when it was most intolerable. You could compare it to nothing else but being in an oven.*

*After we crossed the line, it grew cooler and after passing the Cape of Good Hope, the Captain ran out to the 52nd or 53rd degree south where it was intensely cold. The cold in Ireland could not at all be compared to it. Before and after crossing the line we had some squalls but they did the ship no harm. Their approach was always indicated by the ship's barometer and the Captain could thus be prepared.*

*For about a fortnight whilst doubling the Cape and after while we were running south, we had very rough weather but the ship being so large and such a fine sailor was not much knocked about. She has sailed when under a strong breeze at the rate of 18 knots an hour and off the Cape in 24 hours sailed 350 miles.*

*Our provision was of the very best description. We had flour, butter, raisins and suet to make bread and ovens to bake it in. We had preserved meat which was very rich and nice presented in tins without any salt. We cooked it various ways. We also had soup and "bouile" preserved also in tins which required only warm water to be poured on it to make excellent soup. Our bacon was excellent being all cured in Belfast and we hardly ever tasted salt beef. We*

*had plenty of tea, sugar, rice, oatmeal, spices, peas, pickles
etc. so that as far as eating was concerned we were not
badly off.*

*I stuck to drinking water and indeed it was very good
considering the length of time it had to be kept and we were
provided with lime juice which when mixed with it makes
a very agreeable drink. There was also porter, wine, and
brandy for us—but we did not trouble it very much.*

*I had to teach the children on board three hours in the
day from 10 o'clock until 1 o'clock and again from 3 o'clock
until 4. There were about 80 boys attending.*

*On the 17th Sept. we came insight of Australia and on
the 18th we took in a pilot and entered the bay. On going
in the ship stuck in a sand bank and was not got off till the
19th. We then sailed up the bay and on the 20th cast anchor,
being at sea only 77 days—the quickest passage ever made
from England to Australia.*

Whelan's diet was typical of that served to members of the privileged
cabin and intermediate classes on *Marco Polo*. Steerage passengers, in
contrast, had to content themselves with stewed and salted beef, salt
pork, rice, peas, and dried potatoes, served over and over again. The
emigrants were divided for their meals into groups of about eight
people who usually came from the same extended family or locality.
Groups were allowed, sometimes, to cook pies and soups at the galley
and often they were able to supplement their meals with additional
provisions brought from Liverpool such as biscuits, tea, ham, sugar,
jams, and preserved eggs. For most of the steerage passengers, this
diet, unappetizing and monotonous as it may seem to us, was likely
the best they had ever encountered in their lives.

Several stories about James Nicol "Bully" Forbes have been handed
down over the years, and they now rank among the most cherished and
best-known tales in the annals of the British Merchant Marine. Some
paint a stark picture of a threatening tyrant who, when provoked, could
completely lose his temper and his self-control. Yet stories like these
are often exaggerated as they are told and retold over time by one old
salt to another. Fortunately, a few first-hand accounts of Forbes' actions
have survived in letters and diaries written by passengers on ships he

commanded. Here are a few examples written by two passengers on the second voyage of *Marco Polo* to Melbourne in the spring of 1853. Written at the time the events occurred, they show Forbes employing a wide range of disciplinary measures, from threats to severe physical abuse. They allow us to draw our own conclusions about this quick-tempered sea captain.

By passenger Edwin Bird:

*March 22*
*Our Captain Has given the Band a good Lecture this after noon respecting them getting Drunk of an evening and being Disorderly and if any more comes to His ear, He would Rig up a Plank and send them all adrift. Griffiths which was the Leader was addressed and a more evil fellow there is not on Board the Marco Polo.*

*March 28*
*The Captn whent below last evening rather late. He found two of the Cabin Passengers with the rest of the Gang Drinking their Wine and concocting there for plunder, I have no doubt. He took them by the scruf of the neck and sent them on Deck and after that He began with the Ladies. Swore if He caught either of them on the Poop Deck again He would throw them over Board, and if not quieter than last night He would land them all on the Cape Verd Islands in the morning (which we sighted about 4 O Clock).... One Passenger was lashed to the Rigging this afternoon for not paying His fine.*

By passenger William Culshaw Greenhalgh:

*March 23*
*The Captain came around in the evening to see the lights out, caught one of the Stewards carrying a bottle of spirits for some passengers on deck after hours, for which the Capt got enraged, struck him several times & afterwards abused him shamefully, by striking him with a large glass Ship lamp cutting his face in several places, breaking his nose*

*and giveing him a pr of Blk Eyes, I can assure you he was
a nice spectacle next morning was laid up & unable to fill
his office for some time, he intends to bring the Capt before
the Authorities in Melburn for his brutal treatment, the
spirits was not for himself, but volunteered to fetch it for the
passengers it is the opinion that the Capt was very much in
wrong.*

*May 19*
*Blowing a complete hurricane all night, the appearance of
a complete wreck, the roughest night we have encountered,
the sea roaring and runing mountains high, one of the
sailors put in Irons was so starved & frozen that he could
not move his hands. The Mate afterwards struck him &
jumped upon him, was taken & put in Irons on the quarter*

**Figure 24** This dramatic drawing from 1887 shows how severely
passengers could be thrown about during a storm.

*deck for refusing to get up for his watch at 4 o'clock A.M. was
pulled out of his birth & placed in Irons untill 8 A.M. was
completely frozen & cried like a child, the Capt asked him if
he would submit, he would not answer, he ordered him to be
taken below to remain in Irons & fed upon bread and water,
the poor fellow will be starved to death. Was very hard
treatment, out 67 days.*

Forbes' actions, severe as they were, must be taken in context: as
noted, it was common practice on British merchant ships for captains
to respond vigorously to unruly behaviour from both passengers and
crew members, even if drunkenness was the cause. In the final analysis, peace had to be kept on board and discipline preserved at all cost.
For examples of the possible consequences of lawlessness at sea, we
can turn to first-hand descriptions by passengers of two near mutinies
on *Marco Polo*. The first incident occurred in port in 1854 during the
fourth round trip of *Marco Polo* to Melbourne. The ship was under the
command of a most unfortunate Captain R. W. Wild on that occasion.
The second happened in 1863 when Captain William M. Arnold commanded the ship.

By passenger H. Scofield:

*October 1854
We had a regular Mutiny on Board when in Port Captain
thrashed the 3rd mate, split one of the sailors' head open
with his pistol and challenged all on board to fight. 17 sailors
desserted the ship the same night Captain fired off a cannon
and hoisted lights for the Police next morning he went on
shore 3rd mate "gave him" in charge to Police for thrashing
him Customs people fined him 130 pounds for firing a
cannon in Port and Government Inspectors entered an
action for stoping allowance of our water.*

By passenger Mrs. William Graham:

*September 17, 1863
Quite a scene today with the Captain and crew after the
riotous conduct of last night I must mention also the sailors*

*in the dead of night broke open the store and took a case*
*of ale or rather 47 bottles they left one by mistake so that*
*this morning they were "some of them at least" drunk as*
*ever the skipper called all hands on poop at eight o'clock*
*A.M. commenced to question who were the rioters his*
*investigation was cut short by one of the sailors coming*
*forward and abusing him he challenged the Skipper to fight*
*him the skipper not at once complying with his request he*
*swore he would fight him the first mate or Jamie Bains....*
*The Captain said he would put him in irons "big Jim" said he*
*must put him in irons also the Captain seeing all prepared*
*to mutiny ordered them forward and so ended all the rows*
*of the great line demonstration the results I must say from*
*it were excellent no more drink to be sold to passengers or*
*sailors except a bottle occasionally to married people.*

Unruly and inappropriate behaviour was not limited to male passengers on board *Marco Polo*. On the ship's second voyage to Melbourne in the spring of 1853, Captain Forbes was accompanied by his wife, a common practice among sea captains on long voyages at the time. During the trip, an incident occurred involving the "Ladies," and Mrs. Forbes had to act to assist her husband in resolving the situation. Here is how Edwin Bird, in his usual colourful manner, described the event:

*March 22, 1853*
*There was a tremendous Row last night between the Irish*
*Ladies and some of our Passengers. They came on Board*
*as Widows of Officers and Gentlemans Daughters, But was*
*surprised at Hearing the noise so late. I jumped out of my*
*Bunk and to my surprise one of those Ladies was Swearing*
*away and challenged to fight any man on Board the Marco*
*Polo. It would puzzle even a Yankee to Pick out 6 such gals*
*as we Have Here even in the Argyle Rooms in London. I am*
*at a loss to know what the result will be before our Landing*
*at Melbourne. They are about all night long and some of*
*the moonlight meets are queer ones to tell, I can assure you.*
*The Captain Has, through the advice of His good Lady,*

*for such she has advised him, put up a Notice on the Poop*
*Cabin today that no ladies are to be on Deck after 10 O*
*Clock without being accompanied by their Husbands which*
*of course no respectable Female would do, and Mrs Forbes*
*declared she would not walke the deck if such Lounging*
*about on the Poop was not stopd.*

Despite its large size, sturdy construction, and superior sailing capabilities, *Marco Polo* was not immune to the effects of sudden squalls and storms. As one might expect, the weather was a frequent topic of conversation with passengers and among crew members as they worked together to trim the sails and adjust the rigging to best advantage. Their goal, and the captain's, was to keep as much canvas aloft as possible without unduly endangering the sails, yards, and masts. If they did it well, in a stiff breeze the ship could easily make 350 miles or more a day for days on end and sometimes over 400 miles, noon-to-noon. If not, or if bad weather came on too quickly for them, major damage could occur, and large seas could flow over the ship and down the hatches into the hold. On rare occasions, these large waves could even carry a man overboard with little or no hope of rescue.

Here is a description of an especially severe tropical thunderstorm included by James Stewart in his letter to his father, written in 1857. The ship was at the Tropic of Capricorn when the storm burst upon it:

*About 5 o'clock on Saturday Afternoon (in this quarter*
*nearly dark) the sky to the west became overcast and black*
*clouds came rolling along on the light breeze. All of a sudden*
*the wind died away—the sea became like a sheet of glass,*
*placid and unruffled—and the stillness which pervaded,*
*coupled with the sultriness of the atmosphere, portended a*
*severe thunderstorm which burst over us in all its fury in*
*a short time after. A few large drops were the precursors of*
*a tremendous shower of rain which poured incessantly for*
*upwards of two hours. By and by a streak of lightning burst*
*from the surcharged clouds, lighting up the sky for miles*
*round us, and the thunder growled in the distance. We had*
*no need of candles that night—every one declaring that*
*they had never seen so much lightning at one time before.*

*Flash followed flash with awful rapidity and for a time it*
*seemed as if the heavens was one mass of flame, while the*
*rattling of the thunder gave the whole a terribly grand effect.*
*All hands were ordered out to reef the sails which before*
*were all set and it was surprising to see with what alacrity*
*and willingness they did their duty in such a storm. By the*
*time the sails were reefed and everything made taut, the*
*storm was right over us and it was truly fearful to think on*
*our position. The wind and sea were rising—the rain was*
*pouring in torrents and we were standing ankle deep on the*
*deck—all round was total darkness, so much so that the*
*men carried lamps and save the noise of the elements not a*
*sound was heard....The storm passed away without doing*
*any harm, but you can scarcely realize a thunderstorm*
*peculiar to the tropics by what I have tried to sketch.*

Mrs. William Graham, who had a good sense of humour and obviously was a student of sailing, describes the effects of storms on *Marco Polo* in a different way:

*September 26, 1863*
*Towards mid day a squall threatened it came on too with a*
*vengeance before time could be taken to haul in the studsail*
*main top gallant staysail for a Royal and mizen top gallant*
*sail we had fortunately the old sails which are always used*
*on ships in the light breezes which are expected else some of*
*the masts must have come down...the evening closed with*
*thunder and lightening which continued through the night.*

*October 4, 1863*
*The wind last night continued strong I was awoke on Sunday*
*morning about three o'clock by a tremendous shock a sea*
*struck the ship sweeping over us and down it came like a*
*river into the intermediate fortunately for us we were on the*
*windward side so that our neighbour opposite got the benefit*
*of the volume of water which in a little time caused much*
*annoyance damaging clothes and trunks...a Scotchman who*
*thought all was up with us he bolted out of his bunk to his*

*horror he found himself standing in water almost knee deep*
*uttering a sound more like a howl rather than a prayer...he*
*made for his berth when...turning into the passage leading*
*to his quarters owing to the wet and the leaning over of*
*the ship our friend the Scotchman missed his footing and*
*down he went at a slide on his posterior to the side of the*
*ship righting himself he discovered his clothes floating in the*
*berth with a lot of tin cans.*

*October 7, 1863*
*Change of wind which blew fresher till we had to stow*
*Royals topgallants fore and mizen topsail reefing main*
*topsail and hauling down all staysails except one, wind still*
*increasing scarcely any canvas left up hugging the wind*
*close; falling being the order of the day the poor unfortunate*
*butcher fell and broke his collar bone.*

Passengers confined to a ship for months on end, with little or no communication with the outside world, can easily become bored, angry, and depressed. As well, they can get on each other's nerves, and minor squabbles and annoyances can quickly become major events requiring intervention by those in authority. The captains and owners of *Marco Polo* likely were well aware of this potential problem, and they took active steps to keep their passengers busy and entertained. Band concerts, lectures, mock trials, and amateur theatricals occurred regularly, photographs were taken, and games and books were readily available to pass the time. In warmer waters, small boats were launched and male passengers were allowed to swim and bathe from them. Women, in contrast, had to be content with infrequent bathing in tubs behind privacy screens on deck. Fishing was a common pursuit too, and there are many stories of large fish, even sharks, being landed on board *Marco Polo*, causing much damage in the process (see Chapter 6). There was even a regularly published on-board newspaper called *The Marco Polo Chronicle*, which contained messages from the captain and a variety of stories and poems from others on the ship (see Appendix).

The captain's reports in the *Chronicle* are of interest too since they allow us to imagine for a moment that we are actually on the ship receiving instructions from those in command. As examples, here are two messages that were included in the edition of the *Chronicle* published on Saturday, December 24, 1853, more than half-way through the third voyage of the ship to Melbourne. Captains Charles McDonnell and R. W. Wild led the ship on that occasion. Captain McDonnell provided the general news and instructions, while Captain Wild covered a very specific and delicate matter.

> *Ladies and Gentlemen...*
>
> *Since the date of my last report we have made extra-ordinary progress as a glimpse at the Table of Lattitudes and Longditudes I furnish will at once enable you to perceive.*
>
> *I hope you are now sufficiently accustomed to the sea to be able to keep your legs in any weather. You will require all your new gotten skills in the next fortnight.*

**Figure 25**  A drawing from 1887 of passengers relaxing on deck as a ship passes by.

*We may expect strong winds and heavy seas with severe cold for a week or two. The thermometer stands now at 58 a few days in all probability bring it down to 40...*

*It is of the utmost importance that you keep yourselves warmly clad, as otherwise the sudden transition from extreme heat to extreme cold may be seriously injurious....*

*It is a source of heartfelt pleasure to congratulate you on the healthy state of all on board, I consider this fact peculiarly flattering to the Medical gentleman of the Ship, as well as fortunate for yourselves—A few weeks more of careful forethought and you will I trust have reached your destination without one casualty or case of serious illness on the voyage.*

*I hope you will enable me to record this remarkable fact in Australian Navigation.*

*You will I daresay be grateful to learn that we are now in the Westerly trades and may look with confidence to our progress for some days.*

*We crossed the Meridium of Greenwich on Thursday and we are now in the Indian Ocean.*

*During these days from Tuesday noon we have made upwards of a thousand miles.*

*From Tuesday to Wednesday noon, we made 306 miles, from Wednesday to Thursday noon we made 330 miles, and from Thursday to Friday noon we made 366 miles and we are still dashing onwards in our best style.*

*It appears very evident that our voyage will be one of the shortest ever made to the Australian Colonies by a sailing vessel.*

*I cannot conclude my remarks without expressing a hope that your observances of the customary festivities of Christmas will be tempered by that prudence and Sobriety which have marked your conduct throughout the voyage, and wishing you all a Merry Christmas, I remain with hearty good will, yours very truly,*

*Chas. McDonnell Commander*
*Marco Polo 24/12/53*

*To the Editor of the Marco Polo Chronicle*

*Sir, ...*

*Passengers are requested not to sow any wild oats on the "Marco Polo." Anyone disobeying will be punished most seriously.*

*By order of Captain Wild R. W.*

Christopher Harling was a passenger on *Marco Polo* when it left Liverpool for Melbourne on June 12, 1865, with Captain William Mitchell Arnold in command. During this voyage of ninety-four days, Christopher, probably only a lad at the time, kept a meticulous, easily legible diary which is now in the State Library of Victoria, Melbourne. Although highly repetitive, this diary gives us a superb appreciation of the day-to-day activities of a perceptive *Marco Polo* passenger, likely in cabin class. Christopher usually began his day at about 7:00 A.M. when he squeezed out of his tight-fitting bunk and washed himself, on deck if possible, probably with hot water taken from the galley. He then had his breakfast of tea and hard biscuits, usually supplemented early in the voyage by one of the herrings he had brought along, and later in the transit by porridge with sugar. He then loafed or exercised on the deck and sometimes attended a church service at 10:00 A.M. followed by an hour or two of reading from the Bible or another one of the books he had brought with him.

Dinner, the major meal of the day, occurred precisely at noon, when Christopher, along with his seven mess-mates, sat down to servings they had prepared themselves at the galley. He noted a variety of items available for dinner, such as boiled beef or pork, preserved potatoes, rice, pea soup, pickles, mustard, plum pudding, raisins, and lime juice. After dinner, Christopher had to sweep up, and then he was free to amuse himself as he saw fit in the afternoon. He occupied himself by playing athletic games like leap frog, and by helping the crew by pulling on ropes during sail changes and pumping out the bilge. He probably also joined the sailors in singing capstan and halyard shanties to pass the time as they performed these repetitive tasks on deck. Tea and biscuits were served every day about 5:00 P.M., and Christopher was religiously in bed by 8:00 P.M., no doubt with his diary entry completed for the day.

Selected entries from his diary give us snapshots of life on board *Marco Polo* as he saw it:

> *July 11th Tuesday. I got up at 7 washed myself etc. I then got my breakfast and two more boys took the sweeping then one of the constables brought a paper and put it up it was regulations for cooking. The constables are men who carry the single womens food to the galley; the women not being allowed to come forward of a chain that is put across the middle of the ship.*

> *July 14th Friday. I got up at 7 A.M. & was going on deck to wash but the sailors were throwing water all over the passengers & there was scarcely a passenger but that got a wetting however I managed to get on deck and wash without getting wet....After breakfast the sailors that had never crossed the line before had to be shaved, in order to do this some of the sailors mixed some soot oil & tar together then some of them dressed up in old clothes and coloured their faces: then one of them took a little brush made of canvass & daubed the boys faces all over with the mixture & then took a piece of hoop iron and scraped it off then took them by the heels and dipped them head first into a tub full of water which stood by for the purpose. After they had done this they went round and gathered money...which they spent for ale.*

> *July 21st Friday.... After tea I went on deck and watched the setting sun and sky I thought I never see anything so beautiful in my life; it was Magnificent; It looked like a splendid landscape with mountains and vales here and there intersected with streams and rivers; & studded with trees & shrubs and various other shapes too numerous to be admitted.*

> *August 4th Friday. I rose up this morning at 6 washed etc. As the crew were mostly all engaged aloft several of us passengers went and worked away till breakfast hour. The*

*sea today is fearfully rough, you w'd imagine at times that
the vessel when engulfed between two waves would rise no
more; the sailors think nothing of it but we land lubbers
think it very serious.*

Life on board *Marco Polo* could become awfully monotonous during long stretches at sea without much happening beyond the usual
routine. Accordingly, a simple event such as an encounter with a passing ship could cause excitement and trigger memories of home, family,
and friends. Here is James Stewart's account of just such a meeting and
the deep feelings it awakened among the passengers:

*A cry was raised about noon that a ship apparently
homeward bound was bearing down on us and would sail
close bye us. Letters for home was the desire of our hearts
and great was the rush to pen a few lines for our dear
friends. Just as I came on deck with my note in hand, sure
enough there was the Vessel in full sail some 20 or 30 yards
off our bows. Our helm was put "hard port" which caused
us to stand still while our companion followed our example
and came alongside of us—some 30 yards off. She proved to
be the* Indomitable *bound for London with Emigrants from
Melbourne and the first impulse was to give them a hearty
cheer. This was promptly stopped to enable the Captains to
speak, and so quiet was all round that not one word escaped
us. The rigging of both vessels was black with the Crowds
eager to gain information. The* Indomitable *had passed
the "Commodore Perry" (which sailed a month before us)
just three days before going into Bahia for water. A great
many questions as to the winds and weather were asked
after which the passengers on each ship made the welkin
ring with their loud huzzas. The Captains then waived all
further communication and the Vessels were again set in
motion which deprived us of the opportunity of sending
home letters. Our hearts rose within us as we eyed the noble
Vessel fly away before a wind which would soon land her
passengers on the land of their birth, and the tears rolled
uninterruptedly down our cheeks when our band played*

*"Far far upon the Sea" and "Cheer boys cheer" as a parting*
*Salute, and many rushed down to their berths—I among the*
*rest—to give vent to their pent up feelings. Home! What is*
*it? An Emigrant only knows truly.*

## MEASLES: THE CHILD KILLER

Despite the perilous nature of the voyage to Australia in the mid-nineteenth century, the Black Ball Line and its competitors recorded surprisingly few deaths during the passage. In *Passage to the New World*, David Hollett notes that of about 16,970 emigrants who sailed to Australia from Britain in 1856, only 208 died—a mortality rate of only a little over 1 per cent. Of these, 106 were children under ten. The main reason was that the adult emigrants were usually in the prime of life, free of major chronic diseases, vigorous, active, and well nourished on the ship. Their resistance to disease was high and they usually recovered quickly if they were struck down by infections or trauma. Moreover, they received lime juice daily to prevent scurvy and, of course, there were surgeons on board the larger ships and special hospital accommodations too.

While adults generally fared exceptionally well during the passages, the same cannot be said of infants and children. Susceptible to a host of infectious diseases, especially measles, and weakened by malnutrition and diarrhoea, children, especially babies, died in shockingly large numbers during many of the voyages. The first voyage of *Marco Polo* to Melbourne is a case in point. Of the 327 children on the ship on that seventy-six day voyage in 1852, 52 of them (15.9 per cent) died in an epidemic of measles. As a reference point, the annual death rate from measles in Glasgow in the mid-nineteenth century was running at only about 0.1 per cent of the general population, albeit with marked swings as epidemics swept through. Even in the nineteenth century, a time of high infant mortality, the alarm occasioned by this disaster on *Marco Polo* was so great that the emigration commissioners denied access for a time to very young children on board ships they chartered. In their 1852 report, though, the commissioners did not lay any blame for the deaths on the Black Ball Line, Captain Forbes, the ship's surgeons, or its owners. As we shall see, in the light of what we know today about measles and what they knew then, this was the correct conclusion. The

British Parliament, for its part, was stimulated sufficiently by the incident to pass another in its series of Passenger Acts, late in 1852. This one laid down better standards of accommodation, cleanliness, and health care for the passenger liners, to be enforced by on-board inspections prior to sailing.

Measles, also known as morbilli and rubeola, was first identified as a separate disease from smallpox by Rhazes (860-932). Rhazes was a great clinician who ranks with Hippocrates as one of the original portrayers of disease. Thomas Sydenham, in 1670 and 1692, was probably the first to describe its signs, symptoms, and complications. Peter Ludwig, in 1846, went on to identify other features of the disease, including its periods of incubation and communicability. He also noted that one attack of the disease conferred lifelong immunity and that the spread of the disease could be reduced by isolation of affected patients.

Inoculation with secretions from smallpox patients to prevent smallpox, a practice known as variolation, was introduced in England in 1721 by Lady Mary Wortley Montague. In 1911, John F. Anderson and Joseph Goldberger showed that measles was caused by a virus, and in 1963, thanks to the further work of J. F. Enders and his colleagues, the first live measles vaccine was introduced. This was one of the greatest moments in the history of preventive medicine, since prior to the advent of the vaccine, in the US alone there had been three to four million cases of the disease annually, with an average of 450 deaths. With further refinement, the vaccine turned out to be highly effective, giving immunity to 98 per cent of inoculated individuals with few side effects. Unfortunately, the vaccine has not been used as successfully in the world as one would wish, and it has been estimated that nearly one million children, half of them in Africa, still die of the disease each year.

The surgeons on *Marco Polo* were well aware that in measles they were dealing with one of the most highly contagious diseases. They knew that only one case of unrecognized measles (perhaps in the incubation phase) coming on board from the Birkenhead depot would be enough to ignite a vigorous epidemic on the ship, and they would have quickly recognized the characteristic blotchy rash of the disease and its high fever when it occurred. In a matter of a few days they would have had many very ill children, especially infants, to deal with. These children suffered from complications of measles such as respiratory disease, diarrhoea, middle ear infections, and occasionally even more unusual complications such as encephalitis. They may well have attempted to isolate the early cases, but likely were quickly overwhelmed by the intensity of the epidemic. In fact, there was little they could do that would have been truly effective. They had no anti-viral drugs, and unlike today's physicians, no vaccines to prevent the disease, antibiotics to treat its bacterial complications, or intravenous solutions to treat children dehydrated from vomiting and diarrhoea. They also had little understanding of what would be required to truly isolate a patient affected by a highly contagious infectious agent. Perhaps *Marco Polo*'s doctors appreciated at the time that measles was caused by a minute infectious organism of some sort, but they could only guess what that might be. It wouldn't be until the last third of the nineteenth century that medical researchers gained such knowledge and the sciences of bacteriology and virology truly had their start.

Why was the mortality rate for measles so high on board *Marco Polo*? There are at least three possible explanations. First, a great many of the children on the ship were infants, as passenger J. M. Whelan noted. It was known, even at that time, that the younger the child infected with the disease, the greater the chance of death. Second, the level of hygiene on *Marco Polo* was low by today's standards, so there was ample opportunity for infants to contract not just measles, but also diarrhoea and a host of other infectious childhood ailments. Many could easily be communicated from one child to another in the overcrowded conditions between decks. Third, many of the infants may have come on board in a malnourished state, only to become seasick for days on end as the ship heaved back and forth in the ocean. Their parents and guardians, also desperately nauseous, may well have been too ill and weak to look after them properly.

## *MARCO POLO* MEDICINE

Typically, the surgeons (also called surgeon-superintendents) employed by the Black Ball Line were experienced men who had a medical diploma and were certified by the British Royal College. During their training they mastered courses in gross anatomy (including dissections of human cadavers), chemistry, physiology, *materia medica* (drugs and other remedies), pathology, obstetrics, and various aspects of clinical medicine. They also learned a variety of helpful clinical procedures such as tooth extraction, amputation, the suturing of wounds, the setting of fractures, and the delivery of babies. The medical textbooks of the day, such as James Copland's *A Dictionary of Practical Medicine* (published in 1858), contained extensive descriptions of the signs and symptoms of common illnesses and a great deal on remedies. In fact, it was commonly believed at that time, prior to the advent of the science of microbiology, that infectious diseases originated from a poisonous vapour, or miasma, arising from degenerating animal or vegetable matter or toxic air from the breath of the ill. Of course, the smelly interior of a ship on a long voyage was an ideal repository for such noxious matter, so, by the end of their studies, future ship's surgeons knew just how important it was to keep their ships tidy and as clean as possible under the circumstances.

Besides measles, the surgeons on *Marco Polo* had a great many other medical disorders to deal with. For example, venereal diseases, mainly syphilis and gonorrhea, were common among the crew, especially at the beginning of the voyage when they were fresh from contact with prostitutes. Typhus was always a threat since the infectious agent that causes the disease is carried by infected lice, and lice were everywhere on the ship, particularly in soiled clothing and on the bodies of the unwashed. Cholera, typhoid, and tuberculosis were also threats, as were other diseases caused by bacteria such as whooping cough, some forms of dysentery, and diphtheria. Food handling and storage techniques were still primitive and unsanitary, and food poisoning could strike at any time, without notice. Meat and other staples, stored in casks for extended periods on board ship, often became rancid and poisonous. Also, fractures and other traumatic injuries were common in rough weather when passengers and crew members alike were working on slippery decks, masts, and yards to keep the ship in trim and on course. Should a compound fracture occur, without antibiotics, death could very easily be the result.

On the other hand, the surgeons on *Marco Polo* were dealing with a young and healthy population of travellers, so degenerative diseases—such as most forms of heart disease and arthritis—were almost unknown on *Marco Polo*. And as mentioned earlier, scurvy was not a problem since lime juice was regularly available and the voyages were too short in any case for this vitamin-deficiency disease to become manifest. Finally, the incidence of smallpox in Britain had been significantly reduced by vaccination, and the nutrition on board was good enough to prevent other vitamin-deficiency diseases besides scurvy, such as beriberi.

This was just as well since the medicine chests issued to the surgeons contained only a few scientifically proven remedies. Among the more effective ones were quinine for malaria, opium for diarrhoea, and digitalis from the foxglove plant for heart failure. Mainly present in the medicine chests, though, were a great many lotions, purgatives, patent medicines, oils, and syrups, which could only offer symptomatic relief at best. The surgeons also had at their disposal instrument chests, which typically included a variety of knives, threads, and needles for sewing wounds, an amputation saw, a forceps for extracting teeth, a bougie for dilating the male urethra, and pairs of obstetrical forceps for difficult deliveries. Many surgeons at that time also routinely practiced bloodletting for a host of ailments in the mistaken belief that noxious influences could be removed with the blood. Cupping, or the application of glass cups under vacuum to the skin to draw blood, was common then, and it is very likely that the surgeons had a set of such cups available to them on the ship. Unfortunately, there is no scientific evidence of beneficial effects from either bloodletting or cupping for any illnesses, including those under treatment by *Marco Polo*'s doctors.

Undoubtedly the most important and effective thing the ship's surgeons did was inspecting the ship's interior each day to ensure that it was kept as clean as possible under the prevailing conditions. Passengers like Christopher Harling were assigned to sweep and clean up and their work was checked. The galley had to be kept orderly and clean, and the cooking and eating utensils were washed after each meal. Passengers were encouraged to bathe themselves each day, and to wash their children and clothes using basins. In good weather the hatches were left open and attempts were made to deflect the wind into the hold using canvas baffles. Good ventilation was extremely important given the overcrowded and often fetid, rat-infested conditions below decks, and the surgeons knew it.

All in all, it can be said without hesitation that the surgeons were a positive influence on *Marco Polo* and its sister ships. No doubt they saved many lives, both directly by their ministrations and indirectly by their insistence on cleanliness. The emigration commissioners knew what they were doing when they mandated that surgeons must be on board each and every one of the emigrant vessels. The extremely low adult mortality on vessels sailing to Australia bears that out.

What then, from all the available evidence, would it have been like on board *Marco Polo* in the 1850s and '60s? Imagine many different human dramas unfolding simultaneously within the confines of the ship. Some passengers may have been witness to the miracle of life as a baby was born, while others may have been hard at work desperately trying to save the lives of infants afflicted with measles or other infectious diseases. Most, no doubt, carried on with the routine tasks of the day: sweeping up, preparing meals, and sometimes helping the crew wherever they could be of service. The busy passengers held frequent meetings to establish rules and to discuss the events of the day. School classes were regularly held for the children, and lectures were given on a wide variety of topics for all to attend. Religious services were a staple, as one might expect. In the evenings, many of the passengers found time for music, dancing, readings, and plays. Every once in a while the routine would be punctured by a chance meeting with a passing ship, a violent storm, or some unexpected rowdiness from passengers or crew members. But for the most part the pulse of the ship went on, with one event following another, day after day, for over two months. Then, finally, with their destination reached, the passengers were able to disembark and leave behind what was likely the most memorable period of their lives so far. For most, an exciting new world and a new life lay ahead.

**Figure 26** *Proud Heritage*, a recent painting of *Marco Polo* by Captain C. (Bud) Robinson, shows the great ship running full-out with all sails set.

# Five

# "THE FASTEST SHIP IN THE WORLD"

## SAILING THE GREAT CIRCLE ROUTE

*W*hen *Marco Polo* anchored at the Salthouse dock in Liverpool on December 26, 1852, after a globe-circling voyage to Melbourne and back in five months and twenty-one days, the entire maritime world was stunned. How could a pure sailing ship, built of softwood lumber by colonials in far-off New Brunswick, take the prize as the first ship in history to circumnavigate the earth in less than six months? To both mariners and the general public this accomplishment was truly astonishing. They searched for an alternative explanation. Surely, some thought, the ship had struck a rock or an iceberg and had been forced to turn back part way through its voyage. Yet, there it was at its dock in Liverpool, completely undamaged and proudly displaying a new banner that read, "The Fastest Ship In The World." *Marco Polo* had clearly passed one of the greatest milestones in the rich history of maritime transport, and the ship's captain and crew were responsible. Without a doubt, this was a truly magnificent achievement.

The Black Ball Line was quick to capitalize on *Marco Polo's* success. Many kinds of memorabilia were manufactured and sold, and the triumph was widely publicized in newspapers throughout Britain. Thousands came down to the Liverpool docks to view the former lumber carrier. The names James Nicol Forbes and James Baines became celebrated around the world. The Black Ball Line had scored a huge commercial success, and prospective passengers and freight shippers, in both Liverpool and Melbourne, now flocked to do business with it. A second round-trip voyage to Melbourne was quickly arranged.

On the first voyage to Melbourne, Forbes, on the advice of John Towson, had opted to take *Marco Polo* on the great circle route rather than the longer but more familiar British Admiralty route, which took about 110 days and had been in use for more than seventy years. The Admiralty route carried the ships south to Tenerife, past the Cape Verde Islands, and then across the South Atlantic to Cape Town, where they could re-provision if necessary. They then faced a voyage of thousands of miles along the thirty-ninth parallel and across the Indian Ocean to Melbourne.

This route, which follows a constant compass direction, appears at first glance to be shortest when viewed on a flat Mercator map. However, in the construction of a Mercator map, the grid is kept rectangular, and all the lines of latitude and longitude are kept straight and parallel to each other. In order to accommodate the curvature of the earth while still allowing the map to be placed flat on a tabletop, the grid is stretched progressively moving north and south from the equator, and the scale increases as the latitude increases. The net result is that Mercator maps are very accurate at the equator, but become increasingly distorted and inaccurate as one moves towards the poles. That is why, on a Mercator map, Canada, Greenland, and Russia appear so enormous. Mercator maps, however, are useful for steering a ship on lines of constant compass bearing, since, on the maps, the compass direction between two ports of call is the path of a straight line between them. Gerardus Mercator (1512–1594), incidentally, was a highly inventive Flemish geographer, engraver, and cartographer who used mathematics, a protractor and a compass to figure out his maps. He was the first to call a collection of maps an atlas.

Even though the shortest route between two ports of call appears on a Mercator map to be a straight line, a true appreciation of the shortest distance requires that one view a globe instead. There, a piece of string stretched taut between any two points indicates the shortest route between them. Such a route is called a great circle route; if extended, it would divide the earth into two equal parts while still passing through the two points in question. This route, when transferred to a Mercator map, appears curved, but it remains the shortest distance. For this reason, today's airplane routes for long flights generally do not follow a constant compass direction; if possible, they follow great circle routes instead. (Charles Lindbergh followed a great circle route on his famous flight from New York to Paris and saved 473 miles.)

Towson, who was acutely aware of the benefits of great circle sailing, urged Forbes to make use of it. However, for the journey to and from Melbourne, the great circle route had to be broken up into a series of segments, since it would be pretty well impossible for a sailing ship to follow a continuously curved track over such a long distance. Towson had just published a book of tables to aid navigators following great circle routes, *Tables for the Reduction of Ex-Meridian Altitudes*, which was a great help. But even with the aid of Towson's book, following a great circle route with a large clipper was no easy task. It required a navigator with consummate skill, and a captain and crew able to accurately change the ship's direction (usually every day or two at noon), whatever the weather, to keep it closely on its plotted route. The ship's route also had to take into account ice conditions and the prevailing winds and currents as laid out by Lieutenant Matthew Maury. Accordingly, guiding a big ship like *Marco Polo* on a great circle route over long distances was an extremely complex undertaking, and at that time only master mariners like Forbes had the skill and training required.

Later, in the *Mercantile Marine Magazine and Nautical Record* of 1854, Towson praised Forbes in the following words:

> *In the first voyage home of the Marco Polo, I was struck
> in examining her chart and log, with the great amount of
> nautical skill displayed by her Commander, especially in that
> part of her route which extended from 100 W to the south-
> east trades. In this part of her route, if a line could have
> been stretched over the surface of the earth I do not believe
> Marco Polo deviated five miles from the line in a run of
> 3,000 miles; and this feat of seamanship and navigation was
> accomplished under circumstances requiring every attention,
> and an extraordinary amount of skill.*

Clearly there was much more to Forbes than bombast and bullying.

The great circle route carried Forbes and *Marco Polo* almost directly south from England towards South America. It then took them through the doldrums at the equator to the South Atlantic east of Rio de Janeiro. They then headed south-east and passed about seven hundred miles south of Cape Town to pick up the prevailing winds from the west. The great circle route took them down as far south as the ice would allow into the "roaring forties" and even the "howling fifties." This allowed them to take full advantage of the winds and currents as plotted by Maury. They sailed east in those extreme southern latitudes, "running her easting down" for twenty-five hundred miles, before gradually heading north towards the fifty-mile-wide opening of Bass Strait. From there it was just a short run to Port Phillip Bay and Melbourne.

On its first voyage to Melbourne, *Marco Polo* left Liverpool on July 4, 1852, and reached Melbourne in the record-breaking times of sixty-eight days from the time they lost sight of Liverpool until they sighted Melbourne, and seventy-six days from the Liverpool anchorage to the anchorage at Melbourne. This included four days when the ship covered 1,344 miles. This was a remarkable achievement for Forbes and his crew given that the average time for the voyage until then had been about 110 days. The time saved, however, came at a price: on the great circle route both passengers and crew had to endure the furnace-like weather at the equator and then, just a short time later, the freezing cold of the forties and fifties.

*Marco Polo* arrived at Port Phillip Bay at 11:00 A.M. on September 18, 1852, only to find the harbour crowded with about fifty vessels unable to get underway because they lacked crews. The allure of the gold fields had proven to be too great and it took highly inflated wages to entice any sailors at all to sign on for the return voyage. To make matters worse, celebrating miners had distributed gold nuggets among *Marco Polo*'s crew, causing a near riot. Forbes, to his credit, reacted quickly and had his unruly crew imprisoned until the ship was ready to sail. This quick action saved the Black Ball Line a good deal of money and ensured a fast turn-around time of twenty-four days in Melbourne. While in port, 100,000 pounds of gold dust were placed in the ship's bullion safes for the return voyage and a 340-ounce gold nugget, a gift from the government of Victoria to Queen Victoria, was also loaded.

This incident, in which Forbes cleverly outsmarted his crew, quickly became legendary and has been celebrated in verse and song to this day. One of the most famous of these songs is "Marco Polo," written by Hughie Jones of Liverpool, who was with The Spinners, a highly regarded contemporary British folk group:

*The Marco Polo's a very fine ship,*
*The fastest on the sea,*
*On Australia's strand we soon will land,*
*Bully Forbes can look for me,*
*Gonna jump this ship in Melbourne town,*
*Go a-digging of the gold.*
*There's a fortune found beneath the ground,*
*Where the eucalyptus grow.*
*Marco Polo, the fastest on the sea,*
*Marco Polo, the fastest on the sea.*
*Said the Blackball owner, Mr. Baines,*
*To Bully Forbes one day,*
*"It's up to you to keep your crew,*
*While the gold calls them away."*

*Said Bully Forbes to Mr. Baines,*
*"I have a plan so fine,*
*Leave it to me and then you'll agree,*
*I'm the king of the Blackball Line."*

*Now, when we reached Australia's shore,*
*Bully Forbes he declared, "There's scurvy,*
*Now on this trip you will not leave this ship,*
*Until we reach the Mersey."*

*Now we lie in the Salthouse dock,*
*I'll go to sea no more, sir.*
*I've done me time on the Blackball Line,*
*Under Captain Forbes, sir.*

On its return voyage, *Marco Polo* departed from Melbourne on October 11, 1852, and continued to follow the great circle route back to England. It took the ship south of New Zealand and then across the Pacific to a point close to a hundred miles south of Cape Horn, where icebergs often crowded the waters. From there, the ship sailed north through the Atlantic to its home port of Liverpool. The weather was favourable, and the ship had a swift and uneventful voyage, passing by the Auckland Islands on October 17 and Cape Horn on November

3. When it arrived at the Salthouse dock in Liverpool on December 26, crowds of people were there, anxious to see it and perhaps catch a glimpse of its captain, the newly famous "Bully" Forbes. The return trip had taken just seventy-six days and *Marco Polo* had beaten the steamer *Australia* by more than a week. The entire round-trip voyage had taken only 175 days, including the 24-day stopover in Melbourne. No other ship in history had even come close to that. Indeed, had there been an award in Britain for the fastest and most famous merchant ship of 1852, *Marco Polo* would have won it easily.

To celebrate this remarkable achievement and in anticipation of *Marco Polo*'s second round-trip passage to Australia, a "déjeuner" was held aboard the ship on February 28, 1853. Gathered together on this occasion were the partners of the Black Ball Line, members of the press, and many of the leaders of Liverpool's commercial and marine establishments. Once again, Forbes was the centre of attention and, this time, to mark his magnificent achievements, the Black Ball owners and the merchants of the town showered honours and gifts upon him. According to Michael Stammers, the gifts included a magnificent silver tea service (no doubt sterling) and an elaborate candelabra with an inscription praising Forbes and his accomplishments.

On Sunday, March 13, 1853, *Marco Polo*'s anchor was weighed and its second voyage to Melbourne began. It was a beautiful morning and it must have been a spectacular sight to see the ship towed out to sea by the steam tug *Independence*. Forbes was again in command and this time his crew consisted of about twenty-two seamen, eighteen stewards, seven mates, a boatswain, a carpenter, a sailmaker, three cooks, a surgeon, and six others. Because the Black Ball Line found the ship to be overcrowded on its first voyage to Melbourne, the number of

**Figure 27** Land is sighted. At last, the end of the voyage is near.

passengers on *Marco Polo* for this trip had been reduced to 648. The ship also carried in its hold £90,000 in coins.

Based on *Marco Polo*'s previous voyage, the group on board would have anticipated a swift and relatively uneventful passage and this expectation was reinforced by Forbes' boast to them as they started out that he would "astonish God Almighty" with the sailing of the ship. In fact, despite calms and adverse winds for the first few weeks, the Almighty may well have been astonished, as the voyage was completed in the rapid time of seventy-five days. The ship docked in Melbourne on May 29, 1853. Forbes had sailed it hard with much of its canvas aloft, relying on the ship's innate stability in strong winds. And once again, the passengers had been forced to endure the freezing weather of the deep southern latitudes so that he could keep to the great circle route.

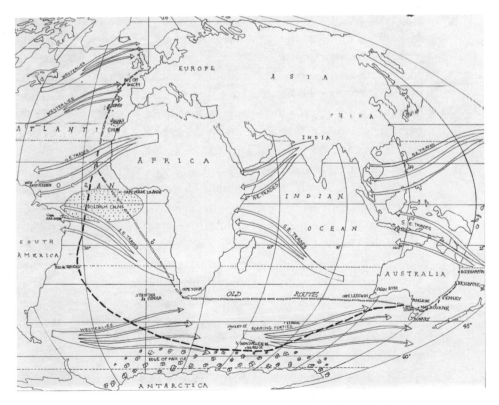

**Figure 28** A map by Don Charlwood showing both the old Admiralty Route and the newer and shorter Great Circle Route.

*Marco Polo's* detention in Melbourne was short once again, and it weighed anchor for Liverpool on June 10, 1853. However, probably due to unfavourable winds, the return voyage took a full ninety-five days and the ship did not reach the Salthouse dock until September 13, 1853. Nevertheless, *Marco Polo's* second voyage around the world had been completed in exactly six months. As well, the ship had made it around the world twice in less than a year, if one includes its detention time in Melbourne but excludes the period it spent in dock in Liverpool between the two voyages. These were remarkably fast times, unheard of to that point, and they heralded a new era in transoceanic transport.

For the third voyage to Melbourne, James Baines assigned a new commander, Charles McDonnell, and a new captain, R. W. Wild, to lead *Marco Polo*. McDonnell had served as chief officer under Forbes, and he was well acquainted with *Marco Polo* and its structure, capabilities, and tendencies. Leaving Liverpool on November 11, 1853, to the cheers of the crowd and the sounds of *Marco Polo's* band and cannon, McDonnell followed the great circle route and reached Melbourne in seventy-two days from its anchorage in Liverpool to its anchorage in Melbourne (sixty-nine days, landfall to landfall). Leaving Melbourne in March of 1854, he returned the ship to Liverpool in seventy-eight days. These were fast times, proving that Forbes wasn't the only one who knew how to get the most out of the ship.

For his part, Forbes, now famous, was given command by Baines of the magnificent extreme clipper *Lightning*, then under construction for the Black Ball Line in Donald McKay's yard in Boston. Forbes immediately traveled to Boston to supervise the final fitting out of the ship prior to its launching on January 3, 1854. Forbes then sailed it across the Atlantic to Liverpool in the remarkable time of fourteen days. *Lightning* went on to make several rapid and dramatic passages to Melbourne and back, the first under Forbes' command in 1854. After serving successfully in the Black Ball Line on the Australian run for many years, it was eventually destroyed by fire at Geelong Harbour near Melbourne in 1869. Fire, of course, was a constant threat to all wooden ships, especially on the open seas where any fire could quickly spread and result in the death of everyone on board.

*Marco Polo* continued on the Liverpool–Melbourne run until 1867, making in total about twenty-five round-trip voyages with surprising consistency. Even though its timbers became more and more strained and waterlogged as time passed, its times remained consistently good, averaging between eighty and ninety days each way. In fact, it completed its final voyage home to Liverpool with the Black Ball Line in only seventy-six days, eight days faster than the large steamship *Great Britain*. Overall, there can be no doubt that during its fifteen years on the Australian run, from 1852 to 1867, *Marco Polo* set a high standard for all other ships to follow. It carried about 15,000 passengers to Australia, had a string of outstanding captains, and pulled off one excellent voyage after another with remarkable regularity over a great many years. All things considered, in its time on the Australian passage, *Marco Polo* ranked among the very best of packet ships, sail or steam. It must have been a very sad day when, in 1867, the ship failed its passenger survey and was forced to go back to its first job, as a cargo carrier.

*Marco Polo's* many voyages back and forth to Australia, however consistent, were not uneventful. It frequently encountered squalls strong enough to damage its sails and rigging, it went aground twice, and it suffered numerous minor collisions. On its second voyage, there was a fire in the galley that, fortunately, was doused in time. On March 7, 1861, *Marco Polo* collided with a large iceberg when in southern waters on its way home to Liverpool and suffered the greatest damage of any of its accidents. The damage was severe forward, but thanks to its stout construction, the ship survived and remained afloat. Leaking badly, it managed to get to Valparaiso, Chile, for repairs, which took from May 2 to May 22. Although no doubt glad to be alive, the passengers had to endure a prolonged passage of 183 days before reaching their final destination in Liverpool.

## "THE FASTEST SHIP IN THE WORLD"

Was *Marco Polo* really "The Fastest Ship In The World" as Forbes and his crew claimed on their return to Liverpool? On the one hand, they had made the round-the-world trip to Melbourne and back in five months and twenty-one days, an absolute and uncontested record. No other ship, sail or steam, had circled the earth nearly as quickly before. But on the other hand, a claim to a speed record of that sort must be substantiated if it is to have any meaning, and today we simply do not know whether *Marco Polo* would have come first in a race with other competing ships of its time, like *Lightning*. Accordingly, the claim to be

"The Fastest Ship in the World" must remain just that, a claim, and a very clever advertising gambit too. Banners proclaiming that the ship was the first to circle the earth in under six months, or the fastest to sail to and from Melbourne, would have been more accurate but probably would not have resonated with the public.

The truth is that with the exception of *Constance*, a New Brunswick–built barque one-third its size, *Marco Polo* was the first ship to follow the great circle route to Australia. Although the voyage of *Constance* was celebrated and widely known, *Marco Polo* showed the way for other large transoceanic passenger ships. Later, several cleverly designed and built clippers such as Donald McKay's *Lightning* and *James Baines*, followed the example of *Marco Polo* and the great circle route and shortened the distance to Australia even further by recording still faster times. Both *Lightning* and *James Baines* were clippers built by Donald McKay for speed as well as beauty, and both achieved record times on the Melbourne run in the 1850s. McKay's ships were unusually long with very sharp entrances, giving them a capacity for high speeds in high winds. Unfortunately, both ships were later destroyed by fire in separate incidents years apart.

How can the great success of *Marco Polo* be explained? Was it simply the right ship in the right place at the right time, or do the men behind the ship deserve the credit for its success? In fact, both explanations are true, as *Marco Polo*'s record-breaking voyages depended on nearly flawless sailing and navigation, as well as ideal weather and other conditions.

Who were the men chiefly responsible for *Marco Polo*'s astonishing performances? First, as we have seen, the ship's success would not have been possible without James Smith's ability to transform the trees of the New Brunswick forest into one of the largest, fastest, and most formidable merchant ships then afloat. *Marco Polo* could not have been better designed or more strongly constructed for the rigours and icy challenges of the great circle route to and from Australia. It could fly with all its canvas aloft in strong winds and seas high enough to deter competing vessels, and it could, and did, hit an iceberg full-on, and survive. It was almost as if Smith knew that the ship was destined to become a record-breaking packet ship on the Australian run.

Second, we must credit James Baines and his partner Thomas Mackay for their shrewdness in recognizing the great promise in that ugly lumber carrier from across the ocean. To their everlasting credit, they appreciated the strength and huge carrying capacity of *Marco Polo*, a clipper with the potential for speed built into its hull. They also knew that the ship was exactly what was needed to help carry the large numbers of gold seekers and other settlers to Australia. Without their involvement, *Marco Polo* never would have had the chance to break records and become famous.

Certainly, Captain James Nicol Forbes must also receive much of the recognition for *Marco Polo*'s success because he was the captain of the ship when it made its record-breaking voyages. Although Forbes was a hard-driving captain with a tendency to tempt fate by forging ahead in rough weather with all sails set, these characteristics were not the main reasons for his remarkable achievements. After all, there were many hard-driving captains in Forbes' day, including McDonnell who succeeded him as captain of *Marco Polo* and who also made fast passages in the ship. Forbes led *Marco Polo* to its triumphs primarily because he was an excellent mariner and, as John Towson attested, one of the finest navigators of his time. Not only was he able to follow the great circle route to and from Australia, making use of Maury's charts of winds and currents, he was also able to keep his ship on its plotted course despite the unpredictable weather and the frequent course corrections required. Forbes also showed wisdom and courage by accepting Towson's recommendation to follow the great circle route in the first place. Forbes, of course, was a colourful character who knew well how to excite the public's interest in himself, the achievements of his ship, and the Black Ball Line. The skilful use of advertising and public relations, by both Forbes and James Baines, no doubt played a key role in the great acclaim granted to *Marco Polo* by the general public.

There is, however, one man who, above all others, deserves the most credit for *Marco Polo*'s outstanding success: John Thomas Towson. Born in Devonport, England, in 1804, the son of a watch and chronometer maker, Towson was drawn to science from boyhood. As he grew older, in addition to an interest in photography, he developed a fascination with geography and the routes taken by ships on transoceanic voyages. He soon came to realize that great circle sea routes were by far the shortest distance between any two ports on the earth's surface, despite the allegiance of mariners to the old, tried and true, Admiralty routes. On the route from Britain to Australia, in particular, he was the first to recognize that following the great circle route could save close to a thousand miles and lead ships to regions where they could benefit from strong and favourable winds and currents as well.

Towson wrote widely on the science of navigation and route selection, and as noted earlier, published manuals and tables on the subject. He also became very well versed in the work on winds, currents, and sailing directions worldwide by Lieutenant Maury. Thanks to his considerable expertise, he was appointed to the post of chief scientific examiner for the Port of Liverpool and also served as secretary for the local Marine Board.

In his various roles, Towson came into contact with a number of Liverpool's famous sea captains, including Forbes, and he spoke to them about the advantages of following a great circle route that made allowances for the prevailing winds and currents as chronicled by Maury. He was the first to call this approach composite sailing. Forbes, to his credit, became convinced early on, thus adding much to the good fortune of *Marco Polo*'s owners. However, it was Towson who originated the idea and he was the one who urged Liverpool's sea captains to apply it.

It soon became obvious to all that by far the most important factor determining the duration of the voyage to and from Australia was the route taken, and this was demonstrated many times over by the huge improvements in times that occurred once Towson's advice was widely adopted and the old Admiralty route discarded. To the delight of all those connected with the ship, *Marco Polo* had the good fortune to be the first big ship to prove Towson's thesis. Of course, other factors were important too. Loading and unloading could be rapid or protracted. A poorly built ship could easily be badly damaged and slowed by a storm. A ship could be becalmed for a long period, or go aground, or hit an iceberg. Many wooden sailing ships were damaged or completely destroyed by fire. An extreme clipper usually would outpace a medium clipper and so on. But, as a general rule, barring obvious exceptions, it was the route that counted the most, and Towson was the one who, more than anyone else, shortened the route from Liverpool to Melbourne and back.

## KEEPING *MARCO POLO* ON COURSE

The navigational skills of Forbes and all the other Black Ball captains of *Marco Polo* accounted in large measure for their ability to keep the ship closely on course throughout its record-setting voyages. They knew

within a few miles where their ship was on their charts, whatever the
time of day or night and wherever they were on the globe. Yet they did
this without the communication networks of today or our dedicated
earth satellites and global positioning systems. Their instruments were
far more basic: a rope to measure speed, a magnetic compass in an
enclosure called a binnacle, and several sextants and chronometers.

Measuring the speed of *Marco Polo* was simple. A rope with knots
at regular intervals was attached to a log, which was then thrown over
the stern of the vessel. The log remained floating in place in the ocean
while the ship moved on and the rope attached to the log was extended
out. The number of knots passing over the stern was counted for a
given time period determined by a sand-glass, and then calculated and
recorded as the speed of the vessel in knots per hour. We still use the
word knots today to refer to the speed of a vessel.

Determining the latitude of the vessel was done with the aid of a
sextant and a chronometer. A sextant is a simple optical instrument
incorporating a telescope, mirrors, and a measuring arc, which can
accurately measure the angle of a celestial body such as the sun or pole-
star above the horizon. The navigators on *Marco Polo* likely had several
such instruments and used them to measure the altitude of the sun at its
highest point above the horizon, at noon local time. This was verified by
reference to a chronometer. Once the sun's altitude was known, it was
then a simple matter to calculate the ship's latitude by consulting tables.
By determining the ship's latitude in this way, the mariners on *Marco
Polo* were following a time-honoured tradition in use by ship's navigators for at least two millennia. Using precursors to the sextant such as
the astrolabe, the quadrant, and the octant, mariners had become adept

**Figure 29** An early nineteenth-
century sextant built by master
instrument maker John Dollond,
London.

over the centuries at "shooting the stars" to determine the altitude of a celestial body above the horizon. Once they knew their ship's latitude, they could then sail north or south to the latitude of their destination, and ride that latitude all the way to port if they wished.

Of course, *Marco Polo* chose to follow a great circle route, so its navigators did not have the option of following a parallel of latitude home. Instead, they needed to know the ship's meridian of longitude as well as its latitude so that they could calculate their exact position at noon each day and then make the appropriate corrections to their course.

Determination of the longitude was done by using the ship's chronometers, one group set to the ship's time and another group set to Greenwich time. For those set to ship's time, sextant sightings determined the exact moment of noon on the ship by measuring when the sun was at its highest point. Those on Greenwich time did not need adjusting since they had been set in Liverpool and were carefully constructed to keep time accurately, within seconds, throughout the entire voyage. The difference in hours and minutes between the two groups of chronometers could then easily be converted to degrees of longitude since the earth rotates through 360 degrees once every twenty-four hours or 15 degrees each hour.

While mariners had been able to measure their latitude at sea easily for thousands of years, the ability to measure longitude had to await the development of accurate chronometers. This advance occurred in England in the mid-eighteenth century. Prior to that, a method involving celestial observation called the "lunar distance method" had been under development by scientists worldwide. Despite decades of work on it, this method ultimately proved impractical for ships at sea, as it required mariners on a bouncing deck to make three nearly simultaneous angular measurements between the moon, the sun or another star, and the horizon. The method proved much more useful on land, where observations could be made from a stable platform and the complex calculations that were required could then be performed at leisure.

The race for a solution to the puzzle of longitude is one of the most interesting chapters in the history of science, and has been admirably documented by Dava Sobel and others. It involves key events in the histories of astronomy and horology, and features, in particular, the inventive genius of John Harrison, perhaps the greatest clock- and watchmaker of all. A watch made in 1753 by England's John Jefferys, under Harrison's guidance and with his specifications, became the world's first practical chronometer suitable for accurately measuring the longitude on-board ships. It contained a number of innovative features including "maintaining power," which allowed it to keep running during winding, and a strip made of two different metals with different heat expansion rates to compensate for fluctuations in temperature. The Jefferys watch was followed in 1759 by an even more sophisticated timepiece, the H-4, made by Harrison himself. Yet the politics and petty jealousies of the time were such that Harrison required the involvement of King George III and the British Parliament on his behalf before a reluctant British Board of Longitude fully recognized his accomplishments.

Harrison's pocket watches and those of his skilled contemporaries were things of beauty, but were far too complex to be copied and produced in quantity. Further simplification and development was required. This was provided in the ensuing decades by two British watchmakers in particular: John Arnold and Thomas Earnshaw. Both produced many pocket chronometers and larger encased box chronometers that were remarkably accurate, reliable, and fully suitable for use at sea. By the end of the eighteenth century, chronometers were widely available and were used to measure the longitude on ships worldwide. Along with sextants, accurate chronometers came down in

**Figure 30** The mechanism of a typical British pocket watch from the early eighteenth century (signed Andreas Zolling, London). Although not accurate enough to be used for the navigation of a ship, it shows the high level of workmanship achieved by British watchmakers of the period.

price over the years, to the point where they could be readily purchased by mariners from shops near the docks. In the nineteenth century, the situation advanced to the point where merchant ships like *Marco Polo* always had several accurate chronometers on board so that they could be checked against each other. In the case of *Marco Polo*, John Towson probably supplied a number of them to the ship's captains since, like his father, he had a special interest in chronometers. Today, Harrison's H-4 watch and several other elaborate timekeepers made by him can be seen in Britain's National Maritime Museum at Greenwich.

There can be no doubt that the achievements of *Marco Polo* marked a genuine milestone in the history of maritime commerce. Few merchant ships before or since have equalled its string of successes over such an extended period of time. Its hallmarks were strength, speed, and consistency on the Australian passage, and it offered its passengers a rapid and safe, if sometimes uncomfortable, transit to the new land.

*Marco Polo*'s success was due to many factors that converged at the same time. Unlike the McKay clippers that came into service shortly after *Marco Polo*, it was not built for speed at the expense of carrying capacity, although James Smith did incorporate some refinements in its hull that separated it from the average lumber carrier of that period and gave it the potential for increased swiftness. Rather, *Marco Polo* was built primarily to carry cargo, and it was only later, after it arrived in Liverpool, that it was converted into a passenger liner.

At that point, one fortuitous event quickly followed another. The advent of the Australian gold rush meant that large numbers of potential paying customers were looking for transportation to Australia. James Nicol Forbes was also available to captain the ship, and he had established himself as a master mariner with few, if any, peers. And most important of all, John Towson was on the scene in Liverpool with his deep understanding of how to set a shorter route to and from Melbourne. At the same time, Forbes and Baines had the courage and skills to adopt Towson's advice at a time when there was no certainty of success with the approach he advocated. Like all great experiments, this was a daring step into the unknown. The fact that the experiment succeeded meant that this small group had achieved a fundamental advance in shipping with the potential to truly improve maritime transport. Thanks to *Marco Polo* and this group, thousands were soon to benefit all over the world.

# THE FINAL YEARS AND
# *MARCO POLO'S* PLACE IN HISTORY

## A MAGNIFICENT SHIP FALLS ON HARD TIMES

*Marco Polo's* second career as a cargo carrier lasted from the time it failed its passenger survey in 1867 until, leaking badly, it was deliberately driven onto the shore by its captain at Cavendish, Prince Edward Island, on July 22, 1883. During that sixteen-year period, when not in ballast, the once proud ship was reduced to carrying a variety of cargoes, ranging from guano to coal and timber, between several widely dispersed ports of call, including Aden, Yemen; Callao, Peru; Rio de Janeiro; Falmouth, England; Quebec City; London; and several others in the Mediterranean.

In 1871, ownership of *Marco Polo* passed from Baines and Company to Wilson and Blain of South Shields, England, who continued to use the ship for carrying coal and timber. In 1874, likely to reduce the number of men needed to sail it, *Marco Polo* was altered to barque rig and had its lower yards shortened by twelve feet. Possibly at this time, it was fitted with the iron mast discovered by divers among its remains at Cavendish. In the early 1880s, with its timbers badly strained and waterlogged, but strengthened by chains wound round its hull, it returned to the North Atlantic trade carrying timber from Quebec to London or Liverpool and returning in ballast. Its times across the Atlantic were usually over twice what they had been during its two maiden voyages, but it continued to provide reliable service until the end. In 1881, it was bought by Bell and Lawes of South Shields, and finally its ownership was transferred to Captain Bull of Christiania (now Oslo) in 1882.

During its final sixteen years as a cargo carrier, *Marco Polo* followed a humdrum routine far removed from the exciting days when it was at its peak as a passenger liner. As its softwood timbers became more and more strained and waterlogged and its worn hull encrusted with marine life, its transit times grew progressively longer. Also, more and more often the ship leaked and had to be fitted with a windmill-driven pump. Sometimes it had to wait an inordinately long time to be loaded. On one occasion in the 1870s, *Marco Polo* and about two hundred other vessels waited over eighteen months in Callao to acquire a load of guano, thanks to a dispute between the Guano Shippers Association and the British shipping underwriters.

Occasionally a rousing event interrupted the dull routine of loading the ship, struggling to the next port, and unloading it. One such event, well remembered and described in detail by Stammers in *The Passage Makers*, concerns a shark that was observed following the ship as it slowly made its way down the Chilean coast en route to Falmouth. The second mate decided to liven things up on that fateful day by catching the shark on a hook, encircling it with a line, and bringing it on board. Not surprisingly, the sixteen-foot shark took vigorous exception to this, and flailing its tail, proceeded to smash its way through the cabin skylight and into the saloon below. Soon the table it landed on was in small pieces along with much of the furniture in the room and some of its very fine paneling. Roused by the tumult, the captain, carpenter, and steward shortly arrived on the scene, and the carpenter proceeded to try to dispatch the shark with his axe. He swung wildly and damaged the deck more than the shark. By the time the shark was finally subdued, the entire saloon was in ruins and awash with slime and blood. Clearly, an exciting time was had by all, although the fate of the adventurous second mate remains unknown.

A second, potentially much more serious incident occurred on June 27, 1883, when a fire broke out on the ship while in port in Quebec. Fortunately, the blaze was quickly extinguished before much damage was done.

On July 19, 1883, *Marco Polo* departed from Montmorency, Quebec, bound for Europe on what would turn out to be its final voyage. Loaded with No. 2 pine in the form of "deals"—lengths of timber sawn from logs at least six feet long—and encumbered by chains wound round its hull to hold its planks in place, it made its way slowly eastward down the Saint Lawrence. In the early afternoon of July 22, while off the north coast of Prince Edward Island, at Cavendish, the ship encountered a furious gale. Leaking badly and with its pumps unable to keep up, *Marco Polo* was in extreme danger. Captain Bull wisely ran it up on shore while he still had some control of the vessel.

## LUCY MAUD MONTGOMERY DESCRIBES THE FINAL DAYS OF *MARCO POLO*

The most vivid and complete description of the demise of *Marco Polo* was written by none other than Lucy Maud Montgomery in "The Wreck of the Marco Polo," a prize-winning essay published in the *Montreal Witness* newspaper in 1891, when she was only sixteen. Montgomery was raised in Cavendish, and is of course the celebrated author of many much loved stories, including *Anne of Green Gables*. Here is her account of the final days of the ship:

> *In writing an essay for the Witness it is not my intention to relate any hair-breadth escapes of my ancestors, for, though they endured all the hardships incidental to the opening up of a new country, I do not think they ever had any hair-raising adventures with bears or Indians. It is my purpose, instead, to relate the incidents connected with the wreck of the celebrated "Marco Polo" off Cavendish, in the summer of 1883.*
>
> *Cavendish is a pretty little village, bordering on the Gulf of St. Lawrence and possessing a beautiful sea-coast, part of which is a stretch of rugged rocks and the rest of a broad level beach of white sand. On a fine summer day a scene more beautiful could not be found than the sparkling blue waters of the Gulf, dotted over with white sails and stately fishing vessels. But it is not always so calm and bright; very often furious storms arise, which sometimes last for several days, and it was in one of those that the "Marco Polo" came ashore.*
>
> *The "Marco Polo" was a ship of the "Black Ball" line of packets and was the fastest sailing vessel ever built, her record never having been beaten. She was, at the time of her shipwreck, owned by a firm in Norway and was chartered by an English firm to bring a cargo of deal planks from Canada. The enterprise was risky, for she was almost too rotten to hold together, she made the outward trip in safety and*

*obtained her cargo; but, on her return, she was caught in a furious storm and became so waterlogged that the captain, P. A. Bull of Christiania, resolved to run her ashore as the only way to save crew and cargo.*

*What a day that 25th day of July was in Cavendish! The wind blew a hurricane and the waves ran mountains high; the storm had begun two days before and had now reached its highest pitch of fury. When at its worst, the report was spread that a large vessel was coming ashore off a little fishing station called Cawnpore, and soon an excited crowd was assembled on the beach. The wind was nor'-nor'-east, as sailors say, and the vessel, coming before the gale, with every stitch of canvas set, was a sight never to be forgotten! She grounded about 300 yards from the shore, and, just as she struck, the crew cut the rigging, and the foremast and the huge iron mainmast, carrying the mizzen-top-mast with it, went over with a crash that could be heard for miles above the roaring of the storm! Then the ship broached-to and lay there with the waves breaking over her.*

*By this time, half the people in Cavendish were assembled on the beach and the excitement was intense. As long as the crew remained on the vessel they were safe, but, if ignorant of the danger of such a proceeding, they attempted to land, death was certain. When it was seen that they were evidently preparing to hazard a landing all sorts of devices to warn them back were tried, but none were successful until a large board was put up, with the words, "stick to the ship at all hazards" painted on it. When they saw this they made no further attempts to land and thus night fell.*

*The storm continued all night but by morning was sufficiently abated to permit a boat to go out to the ship and bring the crew ashore. They were a hard-looking lot—tired, wet and hungry, but in high spirits over their rescue and, while they were refreshing in the inner man, the jokes flew thick and fast. One little fellow, on being asked "if it wasn't pretty windy out there," responded, with a shrug of his shoulders, "oh, no, der vas not too mooch vind but der vas too mooch vater!" Lively times for Cavendish followed.*

*The crew, consisting of about twenty men, found boarding
places around the settlement and contrived to keep the
neighborhood in perpetual uproar, while the fussy good
natured captain came to our place. He was a corpulent,
bustling little man, bluff and hearty—the typical sea-captain;
he was idolized by his crew, who would have gone through fire
and water for him any day. And such a crew. Almost every
nationality was represented. There were Norwegians, Swedes,
Spaniards, two Tahitians, and one quarrelsome, obstinate
little German who refused to work his passage home and
demanded to be sent back to the fatherland by steamer. It was
amusing to hear them trying to master the pronunciation of
our English names. We had a dog called "Gyp" whose name
was a constant source of vexation to them. The Norwegians
called him "Yip," the irritable little German termed him
"Schnip" and one old man twisted it into "Ship."*

*But time passed all too quickly by. The "Marco Polo"
and her cargo were sold to parties in Saint John, N.B., and
the captain and his motley crew took their departure. A
company of men were at once hired to assist in taking out her
cargo and eighteen schooner loads of deal were taken from
her. The planks had so swollen from the wet that it was found
necessary to cut her beams through in order to get them out
and consequently she was soon nothing but a mere shell with
about half of her cargo still in her.*

*One night in August about a month after she had come
ashore, the men who were engaged in the work of unloading
resolved to remain on the vessel until the following morning.
It was wild to think of remaining on her over night, but,
seeing no indication of a storm, they decided to do so. It
was a rarely beautiful evening; too fine, indeed—what old
weather prophets, call a "pot" day. The sun set amid clouds
of crimson, tinging, dusky wavelets with fire and lingering
on the beautiful vessel as she laid to rest on the shining
sea, while the fresh evening breeze danced over the purple
waters. Who could have thought that, before morning,
that lovely tranquil scene would have given place to one of
tempestuous fury! But was so. By dawn a storm was raging,*

*compared to which, that in which the "Marco Polo" came ashore was nothing.*

*The tidings spread quickly and soon the shore was lined with people gazing with horror stricken eyes at the vessel, which, cut up as she was must evidently go to pieces in a short time. One can only imagine the agony of the relatives and friends of the poor men at seeing their dear ones in such danger and knowing that they were powerless to aid them. As the men themselves, they were fully alive to their danger, for they knew that the vessel could not hold together much longer. Their only boat was stuck in by the fury of the waves so that their sole hope of rescue lay in some boat being able to reach them from the shore which, in the then state of the rescue was impossible. In spite of the fact that the boat was full of water three of the men insanely got into it and tried to reach land. Of course the boat was instantly swamped and the men left struggling in the water. Two of them managed to regain the wreck in safety, but the third, a poor Frenchman called Peter Buote, was drowned instantly and, several days after the storm, his body was picked up some distance away.*

*The horror-stricken onlookers still kept their eyes fixed on the fated vessel, in horrible expectation of the inevitable catastrophe; suddenly a cry of horror burst from every lip as the ship was seen to part at the fore-castle head and at once go down. The next minute, however, it was seen that the windlass and a small piece of the bow still remained held by the anchors, and that the men were clinging to this. With the courage of desperation, several attempts were now made to reach the wreck but all the boats filled with water and were compelled to return. Nothing could now be done till the storm would abate and it was only one chance in a hundred that the fragment would hold so long.*

*Meanwhile the beach was a sight to behold; the vessel having broken up, the planks in her washed ashore and for miles the shore was piled with deals and all sorts of wreckage till it was absolutely impassible!*

*At last, towards evening, the sea grew a little smoother, and though the attempt was still fraught with much danger, a seine-boat was procured and a party of brave men went to the rescue. They reached the wreck in safety and hauled the men on board by means of ropes. Thus they were all brought safely to land, exhausted with cold, wet, and hunger, but still alive. What rejoicing there was when they were safely landed, and, as the kindly neighbors crowded around with that "touch of nature that makes the whole world kin", there was joy indeed except among the poor Frenchman's relatives, who were mourning the loss of their friend.*

*About a week afterward, in another gale, the last vestige of the vessel disappeared and that was the end of the famous "Marco Polo", celebrated in song and story, her copper bottom, chains, anchors, etc., in all, it was said, about $190,000 are still there, and, though almost buried in the sands, in a clear calm day the little fishing-boats sailing over the spot can discern, far beneath the remnants that mark the spot where the "Marco Polo" went down.*

## HONOURS AND TRIBUTES

Nowhere is *Marco Polo* better remembered than in the city of its birth, Saint John, New Brunswick. In Saint John, a small group of dedicated citizens led by schoolteacher Barry Ogden has been working for over fifteen years on a variety of projects designed to immortalize the ship. Their efforts have been mainly focused on gaining financial backing and approvals to construct a large-scale replica of the ship and site it

**Figure 31** Barry Ogden's dream of a replica of *Marco Polo* on the Saint John waterfront appears now to be headed to fruition. He is shown here in a 2003 photograph holding a drawing of the replica.

on the city's waterfront. Placed there it would be both a major tourist attraction and a vibrant memorial to Saint John's illustrious shipbuilding past. This project appears now to be headed for success, albeit with a smaller replica.

Besides the drive for a replica, the ship has also been remembered in Saint John in many other ways. For example, local musician and composer Jim Stewart has written and recorded a suite of music celebrating *Marco Polo* and, with the involvement of many others, has mounted a marvellous folk opera about the ship. Here are the rousing lyrics to Stewart's "Marco Polo":

> *Where the Marsh Creek waters meet Courtenay Bay*
> *(Heave her round and let her fly)*
> *James Smith's yard a keel did lay*
> *(There's no ship here can match her)*
> *She was launched with a groan and thud*
> *(She's like a demon sailing by)*
> *She's stuck two weeks in the Marsh Creek mud*
> *(There's no ship here can catch her)*
>
> *Chorus:*
> *And it's Liverpool in fifteen days,*
> *The seven seas her name will praise;*
> *The wind in her hair and her sails unfurled,*
> *She's the fastest ship in all the world*
> *And her name is Marco Polo*
>
> *Her keel's all bent she'll never sail (Heave her round...)*
> *James Smith's hopes are doomed to fail (There's no ship...)*
> *She's felt the wrath of jeers and scorn (She's like a demon...)*
> *Through the pain the legend's born (There's no ship...)*
>
> *Chorus*
>
> *To the Black Ball Line she soon was sold (Heave her round...)*
> *Australia bound in search of gold (There's no ship...)*
> *She was ruled with an iron hand (She's like a demon...)*
> *When Bully Forbes was in command (There's no ship...)*

*Chorus*

*It's sixty-eight days to Melbourne town (Heave her round...)*
*The waves will echo her renown (There's no ship...)*
*She's beating packets run by steam (She's like a demon...)*
*From James Smith's wish to Saint John's dream (There's no ship...)*

*Chorus*

*For thirty-two years she ran the tide (Heave her round...)*
*On Cavendish shoal she finally died (There's no ship...)*
*But dreams are much too hard to kill (She's like a demon...)*
*The Marco Polo's living still (There's no ship...)*

*Chorus x2*

As well, the National Film Board of Canada has produced a short film on the vessel, and Tony Arseneau of Saint John has created an interactive and informative website on the history of the ship. Other remembrances include a federal monument dedicated to the ship in Saint John, a CBC radio play, a high school musical, and a float celebrating the vessel in a Saint John parade. This ship truly was, and still is, the pride of New Brunswick.

Other tributes to the ship have had both a Canadian and an Australian context. Harlequin romance writer Flora Kidd, a resident of New Brunswick, has written two engaging novels featuring the ship entitled *To Hell Or Melbourne* and *Until We Meet Again*. Also, the Royal Canadian Mint has issued an attractive $20 sterling-silver coin to mark the 150th anniversary of *Marco Polo*, and both Canada Post and Australia Post have issued commemorative stamps featuring original paintings of the vessel. The images of *Marco Polo* on both the Canadian stamp and coin were done by Canadian artist J. Franklin Wright.

Because of its fame and unusual appearance, *Marco Polo* has also been a favourite subject for model builders all over the world. One of the best of these can be viewed in the New Brunswick Museum in Saint John and another, also superb, can be seen in the Merseyside Maritime Museum in Liverpool. As well, a hot air balloon with a large picture of *Marco Polo* on it has appeared regularly in the skies over Saint John.

A number of bits and pieces of *Marco Polo* have survived all of the years from its wreck to the present. Among these, one can find in the New Brunswick Museum a brass telescope, a carving of Marco Polo himself from the ship's stern (see page 23), a dinner bell, and a forty-five-ton cast-iron anchor. Other pieces were obtained from the wreckage of the ship by Cavendish residents at the time it went under, and it is said that some of these can be found to this day scattered in homes and businesses throughout the Maritimes. Many of these articles were probably purchased at the wreck sale that was held on Prince Edward Island in August 1883. At the auction, the cargo was sold for £5500 and the wreck for £600. The stove and steering apparatus were subsequently transferred to the new barque *Charles E. Lefargey* of Charlottetown.

Finally, *Marco Polo*'s underwater remains have been explored and charted by divers with Parks Canada, and its resting place has been designated a Federally Protected Site. The divers' survey has revealed a great deal about the ship, although there is much more to be uncovered. Still visible to the divers were segments of the ship's backbone, including parts of its keelsons, two sections of its iron mast, its anchor chain, and portions of its decking. The wreckage lies in shallow water, and today it is an important feature of Prince Edward Island National Park.

## THE FATE OF JAMES SMITH AND SON

As for shipbuilder James Smith, his prosperity reached its peak with the construction of *Marco Polo*. In February 1852, Smith transferred all sixty-four shares to his son, James Jr., and seemed to run into some bad luck with his other ships. At least one, *Unicorn*, was still owned by him when it sank with passengers on board while travelling from Liverpool to New York in 1851. Nevertheless, from the 1830s to the 1850s, the decades in which he was active, Smith's ships lasted longer than those of any other Saint John shipbuilder, averaging over eighteen years of working life on the high seas.

In 1854, Smith began encountering several major obstacles to his ship construction business. One key concern was the cost of ship insurance, which was controlled by the giant Lloyds combine. Two ships, *Matias Cousino* and *Euroclydon*, were given a six-year rating by Lloyds instead of the usual seven, because of the use of pitch-pine for their transoms. (Pitch-pine is a name given to several species of pine which have especially resinous wood.) Smith vigorously objected, but the lower rating was upheld, dramatically increasing insurance costs and reducing the value of the ships. Adding to Smith's misfortunes, another ship, *Biblio*, was badly damaged in launching. To make matters still worse, a serious fire on April 28, 1855, consumed a new ship still on the stocks in Smith's yard, as well as the rigging and a variety of stores. The fire had started because Smith had built a steam-box, or perhaps even a steam-driven sawmill, that was placed too close to the ship under construction. Apparently the door to the firebox was left open, shavings were ignited, and the whole yard caught fire while the builders were at dinner. Smith, who was chronically under-insured, lost $22,000 in this disaster and may well have been seriously discouraged since only one remaining ship, *Burita*, was registered in his name in his lifetime.

James Jr. carried on doggedly and built ships under the Smith name until about 1865. James Smith Jr. then changed careers—in his declining years, he worked as a clerk for the European and North American Railroad Company.

James Smith, one of the greatest wooden shipbuilders in Canadian history, died in Woodstock, New Brunswick, in 1876 at the age of 73, probably of pneumonia. His obituary, published the day after his death in the Saint John *Daily Telegraph*, recognized Smith for the contribution he made to shipbuilding and industry in New Brunswick, noting that "his energy and skill have made New Brunswick known all over the world as deservedly celebrated for building famous clipper ships, beautiful in appearance, fast sailors and large carriers. Mr. Smith was much and deservedly esteemed in all his relations in life." Today, Marsh Creek is spanned by Saint John's busiest bridge, appropriately named after *Marco Polo*.

## MARCO POLO'S PLACE IN HISTORY

There are a great many reasons why *Marco Polo* deserves to be remembered as one of the finest of all sailing ships. Cleverly conceived and built in New Brunswick by James Smith to be a humble lumber carrier, it absolutely astounded the entire maritime world when, in 1852, it carried almost 1,000 people from England to Australia in record time. And this was not all. On its return to England it became clear that the time for its entire globe-circling voyage was also a record. One can imagine the utter amazement throughout the merchant marine and in Saint John, Liverpool, and Melbourne when these facts became known. *Marco Polo* had become a world champion, and the prize possession in James Baines' small but quickly growing Black Ball fleet. These achievements alone are enough to secure *Marco Polo* an important place in maritime history.

But there is much more. After its initial record-breaking circumnavigation of the earth, *Marco Polo* went on to become the mainstay of the Black Ball fleet, reliably carrying passengers on the Australian run for many years. For a considerable time, it set the standards for all ships on the passage, and it also introduced the great circle route to the Black Ball and competing lines as the shortest and fastest way for ships to get from Britain to Australia and back. Captains on many other ships on the passage drove their ships hard in an attempt to follow *Marco Polo*'s example and emulate its achievements. In its role as a passenger ship, it carried many thousands of emigrants from Britain to a new and productive life in Australia. In doing so, it played a key part in the growth of the new colony and an important role in the saga of the great Australian gold rush.

In addition, *Marco Polo* played on an immense stage and its magnificent accomplishments were news all over the globe. Many thousands followed its exploits in the newspapers of the day as it sailed from port to port. Thousands also lined the banks of the Mersey and cheered the ship on when, with its band playing and its flags flying, it left on another of its many voyages to Melbourne.

A good part of the reason for the great interest in the ship, then and now, rests on the fact that its principal owner, James Baines, and its first captain on the Australian passage, James Nicol "Bully" Forbes, easily rank among the most colourful and interesting characters in the entire history of the British merchant marine. Baines, the aggressive, high-rolling entrepreneur, and Forbes, the clever, aggressive, and boastful captain, were a superb combination, especially when teamed with *Marco Polo*. At the time, crew members and passengers alike were well aware of this and they became fascinated with the rapidly unfolding story of the ship.

All things considered, there can be little doubt that *Marco Polo* readily places among the most fascinating and celebrated of all large sailing vessels. It was a remarkable clipper, and one that fully deserves a prominent place in the story of Britain's merchant marine and in the histories of Canada, the United Kingdom, and Australia.

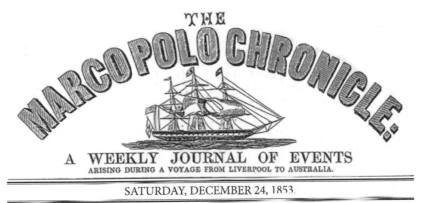

# SELECTIONS FROM
# THE MARCO POLO CHRONICLE

## THE MARCO POLO CHRONICLE.

### A WEEKLY JOURNAL OF EVENTS
ARISING DURING A VOYAGE FROM LIVERPOOL TO AUSTRALIA.

SATURDAY, DECEMBER 24, 1853.

CHRISTMAS IN THE INDIAN OCEAN.

Christmas is with us once more. Hoary kind old Christmas, the Sabbe of the year. In all minds there are fond associations with this festive season on our island home by many a cheerful fireside while the Yule log burns brightly on the hearth.... Families are reunited, hearts estranged by worldly tasks and cares through the live long year now warm towards each other. Friends sundered by travel and divers interest meet now to share their joys and learn to forget their sorrows.

Soilworn artisans gather their families about them, and are made happy, they have struggled long and hardly through the year, sunrise has found them at their toil and midnight has surprised them fagging at the work bench.

Still they have looked onward with pleasurable anticipation to the joys of Christmas like the storm tossed sailor to the beacon that speaks of safety and the wished for period has arrived.

The loved and loving are assembled; fond faces that have gladdened their energetic souls in trial and adversity now share their mirth around the festive board.

Old age enjoys the hour with peaceful smiles.

Youth mingles in the sport with boisterous merriment.

Sorrow is banished save when thoughts are turned to the absent. Then all hearts yield their sympathies to those who erstwhile share their happenings.

In such circles we are remembered. A thousand fancies haunt their teeming minds fair would they penetrate the mystery of our whereabouts and the manner and means of our enjoyment for none shall doubt that we will make our

Christmas joysome and in the deepest recessed of young and trusting hearts tender thoughts well up though silent, wonderful prayers are urged for the far off wanderer on the mighty deep.

There is ecstatic pleasure in the thought. Our blessings on them all right-heartily. Do we reciprocate their kindness. May Christmas be joyous to their hearts, may our reunion be speedy and cloudlike, and may our own happiness be ever tinctured by the pleasant consciousness that we are remembered.

Kind readers, a Merry Christmas to ye all.

## NEWS OF THE WEEK.

An accident that may have proved fatal to our esteemed chief officer, Mr Oxner occurred at an early hour on Wednesday morning.

The hands were engaged setting the top gallant studding sail, it was blowing very strong at the time when the sheet carried away taking Mr Oxner with it. For some few seconds he was in imminent danger of drowning but calmly watching his opportunity he loosed his hold and fell across the top gallant sail. We regret to add that he was severely bruised by the fall.

The curious in ornithology have had an abundant opportunity of indulging their predilection during the first week. Mother Carey's chickens, better known as Stormy petrels, have been frequent visitors. Cape hens and Cape Pigeons have been very numerous, and fine specimens of the majestic albatross encircle us rising and swooping in all directions in glorious style....

## SPORTING INTELLIGENCE.

A sweepstakes of Ten Guineas was made up in the Saloon on Tuesday to be decided by the day of our arrival inside Port Phillip Heads. There were twenty one subscribers and the dates of tickets issued extends from 13th Jany [January] to 2nd February inclusive.

The betting fever has prevailed with great violence during the week, heavy odds have been given and taken as to time of arrival. One bet of some consequence has been made that we shall enter Port Phillip heads within 64 days from Liverpool. The general impression is that our voyage will not far exceed seventy days from Liverpool....

*Printed by meticulous Autographic Press.*

# THE MARCOPOLO CHRONICLE.

## A WEEKLY JOURNAL OF EVENTS

ARISING DURING A VOYAGE FROM LIVERPOOL TO AUSTRALIA.

### SATURDAY, JULY 29, 1854.

#### TO OUR READERS.

The owners of the Black Ball Line of Australian Packet Ships, with a liberality of the most extreme kind, have afforded us the opportunity of representing the fourth estate of the realm in a new and singular field for such a duty. The fame of the Marco Polo has become a household word, and its career is a matter of general interest. We shared in the concern which was prevalent when the account of the stranding of the noble ship reached England, and we experienced a corresponding amount of pleasure when, at an almost simultaneous period, the favourite vessel arrived safely—and almost soundly—in the Mersey, a proof of her seaworthy qualities. The Marco Polo has been in many respects a fortunate ship: fortunate in herself, fortunate in her commanders, and fortunate in her officers. Although the owners of the Marco Polo had the consolation upon receiving intelligence of the loss of their renowned vessel of what is called full insurance, we are assured that they were far better satisfied when they again saw her safely in the port of Liverpool than they could have been if they had received at the hands of the underwriters her nominal money value. The Marco Polo has so far proved a prize in the midst of a host of blank ships, and her popularity will not, so far as human endeavours can avail, be allowed to decline.

The re-fitting for the present voyage proves the truth of our assertion. Already has her gentlemanly commander, Captain WILD, gained the esteem and praise of the passengers, one and all: the ladies say, "what a nice man the captain is;" the gentlemen aver that "he is a trump," and a few of the male sex, still more enthusiastic, vow that "he is a regular brick!" Each of these expressions of good will have their peculiar significations, but they may be all voted as deserved compliments. The chiefs of every department enjoy a fair share of the good expressions of public opinion; the chief mate, chief steward, and chief cook, are, as far as we can judge, all that can be desired. The stewardess, Mrs. TURNER, deserves especial commendation; her marked attention to the duties of her arduous situation, and her feeling and praiseworthy attendance on the sea-sick invalided lady passengers, are worthy of our highest admiration. We might extend these encomiums of praise to the other officers of the vessel; but it will be sufficient to say that under the present management there is every prospect of good order and a considerable amount of good humour. Now this satisfactory state of affairs is, in our opinion, but so much evidence of the desire of Messrs. JAMES BAINES & Co. to keep up the name of the firm for unparalleled liberality, If this desire did not exist we are quite sure that a complete printing office and an editorial and reporting staff—ahem!—would not have formed a portion of the equipment of the gallant Marco Polo. Having said so much for the firm, the ship, the captain, and the officers, it becomes our duty to give some account of our intended operations. The MARCO POLO CHRONICLE will, weather and health permitting, be issued every Saturday during the voyage.

A sufficient number of copies will be circulated gratuitously in every part of the ship for the general perusal of the passengers; but should there be a desire on the part of any of our readers to possess themselves of a complete series of our ocean newspaper we shall be happy to enrol their names on the payment of the fee of one shilling. We are compelled to adopt this secondary plan of disposing of the CHRONICLE in consequence of the absolute impossibility of extending its free circulation to the individual members of the large community of our floating home. No reasonable objection can be urged against this arrangement, and at any rate we may in truth defy competition.

It has been asked what we shall find to say in this novel newspaper, when there is scarcely any possibility of obtaining intelligence of the Russo-Turkish War, or the sayings and doings of our Imperial Parliament, or the Crimes, Accidents, and Offences, which help to fill up the journals in Old England. We are somewhat at a loss for a reply, for we cannot look into futurity; but we may reasonably hope for a variety of incidents during the voyage of sufficient interest for the columns of the CHRONICLE. We do not, however, hope for casualties; but would rather prefer to record events of a more pleasing nature. We are open to correspondence and communications upon such subjects as will be likely to interest our readers generally. Advertisements will be inserted at an unusually low price, and as there are doubtless numbers of persons who have their "wants," they will be thus afforded the opportunity of obtaining what they desire. By this means surplus articles or

stores may be disposed of, and we cannot see any reason why some few industrious tradesmen may not find profitable employment for the time which may otherwise hang so heavily on their hands. In fact it is intended that the MARCO POLO CHRONICLE shall answer to the community for whose amusement and convenience it is issued all the purposes of an ordinary newspaper....

---

### MISCELLANEOUS MATTERS.

Some of the first-cabin passengers shot a large sun-fish before breakfast time on Thursday morning.

On Thursday morning an attempt was made to communicate by signal with a vessel, which was evidently homeward bound. The saucy craft declined the act of civility!

Two or three immense shoals of porpoises were seen sporting in the water on Wednesday. Some of the sportsmen on board prepared their firearms, but the game were too many for them....

A RUNAWAY HUSBAND.—About a week ago Captain Wild received a letter dated "Pittington, July 17th, 1854," informing him that there was a probability of one of the passengers on board the Marco Polo (whose name we forbear to mention) being removed before the sailing of the vessel by a policeman. The reason assigned was that he had illtreated his wife, who lay dangerously ill. We hope that a week on the ocean has afforded the fellow sufficient time for advantageous reflection upon the brutality of his conduct.

A FORTUNATE "STOWAWAY."—About twelve o'clock on Sunday last some little excitement was occasioned on board by the announcement that a "stowaway" had been found on board and a fine specimen of the genus was duly ushered on the quarter-deck. The uninitiated soon found that a "stowaway" was a slender youth of about 18 years of age, who had hid or stowed himself away in the lower hold, with the intention of obtaining a free passage to the

Antipodes. The young gentleman gave his name as Josiah Thomas, and he was pretty considerably disconcerted when the second mate made his appearance with a few sets of steel bracelets,—*vulgo* "handcuffs"—which were not, however, made use of, a promise having been exacted that he would keep station on a hencoop on which he had been perched. His disconsolate countenance procured him the sympathy of several of the first cabin passengers, who made a tolerable subscription for him, in order that he might not be landed penniless in Liverpool, to which place it was intended he should be returned by the tug Tartar, which was then towing us along. About one o'clock it was made known that one of the second cabin passengers, who had left his wife and family "in a huff," was desirous of returning to Liverpool and forfeiting his berth in favour of the aforesaid Josiah Thomas. Captain Wild consented to this extraordinary arrangement and at midnight the repentant husband left the ship, and would, we are sure, be warmly received by his family.

ANOTHER STOWAWAY.—On Monday, too late for any chance of returning the young gentleman home another "stowaway" was discovered on board, who had rather a wicked kind of countenance—one of the old offender sort. This youth was duly installed as an assistant in the hospital, where it is to be hoped his duties will be of a light nature.

A FUNERAL AT SEA.—The passengers on board the Marco Polo had an opportunity of witnessing a funeral at sea on Thursday last, the body of the poor infant mentioned in our obituary being consigned to the deep with all becoming ceremony and solemnity. The Rev. Mr. Hannay (one of the chief cabin passengers) read the funeral service in a most impressive manner, and afterwards delivered an appropriate and feeling address.

SANITARY REGULATIONS.—A meeting was held on Tuesday last for the purpose of promoting good order and regularity on board…. The following rules were adopted:—1. That the committee should meet the chairman at the capstan head at half-past ten every morning, for the purpose of making a personal inspection of the "between decks." 2. It is especially requested that any complaint will be made to the aforesaid committee from which it will be represented (if necessary) to the chairman, who will report it to the captain who will investigate the matter. 3. The committee is authorized to suppress any malpractices, such as gambling, swearing and obscene conversation, as much as lays in its power, and to report the same if such practices are continued after due caution. 4. There having been great complaints of passengers being disturbed after the hour of ten at night, it is requested that such disturbances will be discontinued, or the offender will be reported and punished at the discretion of the captain. 5. It is requested that any person detecting another deviating from the general rules will at once report the same to the committee.

# THE MARCO POLO CHRONICLE.

## A WEEKLY JOURNAL OF EVENTS
### ARISING DURING A VOYAGE FROM LIVERPOOL TO AUSTRALIA.

### SATURDAY, AUGUST 12, 1854.

PROPOSED REPRINTING OF THE FIRST
NUMBER OF THE MARCO POLO CHRONICLE.

The MARCO POLO CHRONICLE has been circulated on board to an extent far beyond our first intentions, but yet there are still many persons on board who will be unable to possess themselves of such an appropriate, and, we hope, interesting memento of the voyage. The point where we were compelled to "draw the line" was the number of sheets of paper, divided by ten; provided for the whole of the second series of this journal. In other words, a calculation was made for ten weekly issues of the CHRONICLE, and a liberal distribution thereof was provided for, free of all expense to the passengers. But as it was rightly conceived that many parties would like to be ensured complete files of the CHRONICLE, we adopted the plan of registering the names of such persons on payment of one shilling. By this means every copy of the paper was bespoke in advance of its publication; since which we have been sorry to find that there are some parties who are so much disappointed, that they have been heard to declare that they would like the CHRONICLE "at any price!" We have succeeded in obtaining paper sufficient for about TWENTY more complete sets of the CHRONICLE, and it is our intention to *reprint* No.1, provided the aforesaid copies are in request at five shillings for each series. This is the lowest rate which can be fixed upon as being sufficient to compensate us for the additional labour which will thus be required from us on the completion of the task we have undertaken. The only mode of distribution of this extraordinary edition of the CHRONICLE will be the very fair one of " first come, first served."

WHAT WE ARE DOING ON BOARD
THE MARCO POLO.

When we last had the pleasure of addressing our readers, we were making fair but not rapid progress towards the distant port of Melbourne, in the prosperity of which most of our readers, whatever their several pursuits, hope to share. We were encouraged to hope that as we had made a fair start, there was some prospect of a satisfactory termination to the voyage which we have undertaken. Since then, however, although we have had, upon several occasions, evidence that we were leaving Old England in the distance at the rate of from eight to ten miles per hour, we have also had the mortification to hear that the heaving of the log only showed that we were progressing, what are technically called by seamen from three to four knots, but which will be more generally understood by landsmen as miles—or something like three, rather more, we believe—per hour. *Nil desperandum.* If we are not going very quickly, we are going as merrily as can well be.

What with singing, dancing, gymnastics, shooting, and other exercises, the passengers on board, whether of the first, second, or third class, are all bent upon making the best of their bargain. They have undertaken a voyage from one side of the world to the other, and they must, of course, be prepared to spend the rather lengthy period occupied in its performance in as pleasant a manner as possible. Monotonous as a sea voyage may be to some persons, there are others who look upon novelties every day. A brilliant sunset, the rising of the silvery moon from the apparent boundary of the wide expanse of ocean, the shooting stars or meteors, the shoals of porpoises, an occasional flying fish, the distant vessels, the ever rolling ocean; all these have their peculiar charms, and, mingled with the hope of a prosperous future, enable some hundreds of souls not only to endure, but to enjoy life on shipboard....

The various islands and places passed during the voyage excite some degree of curiosity as to the peculiarities and products thereof; the last few days has been particularly fruitful in this respect. We have passed the Madeiras and the Canary Islands, and are fast approaching the Cape de Verda. We have also got into rather warm quarters, for, during Wednesday night we found ourselves within the Tropics. It must not, however, be supposed that we have arrived at the highest point of heat which we shall have to endure; there is yet a latitude to be passed where our powers of endurance will be taxed to the fullest extent. It is our intention to give brief descriptions of the places passed in that portion of our journal devoted to "Miscellaneous Matters."

We have been pleased upon several occasions to see the partiality of the numerous passengers onboard from Scotland for their national music. The piper,—who, by the by, is a merry-looking young man,—seems to be quite a favourite with his countrymen, who march after him much in the same manner as their sires of old followed their leaders to the battle field. In noticing the circumstance of a piper being on board on a previous occasion, we spoke of " the discordant sounds of the bagpipes," and it has occurred to us that we may have been suspected of an intention to insult the Scotchmen in thus showing disrespect to their national musical instrument. Now, we beg to assure our Scotch friends that we are ardent admirers of their character, and have the highest respect for the tastes of all our readers, whichever may be the portion of our beloved Queen's dominions that gave them birth. Dr. Johnson once said that "of all our noises music was the least disagreeable." Our opinion of the bagpipes may be thus expressed:—Of all music the bagpipes are the least grateful to our ears. It may be a lack of musical judgment that has led us to this conclusion, and at any rate we will willingly submit to have our musical taste questioned rather than lie under the implication that we have given intentional offense to any of the passengers of the Marco Polo, for whose information and pleasure it is our highest source of gratification to cater.

## MISCELLANEOUS MATTERS.

MEDICAL REPORT.—During the week diarrhoea has been rather prevalent, the effect of the hot weather....

BOTTLING THE PLEDGE.—We have been informed that when the Marco Polo was off the Canary Islands, the carpenter, sail-maker, and boatswain's mate, took the teetotal pledge, which they deposited in a soda water bottle,—emblematical of their future refreshment—and then threw overboard....

THE CANARY ISLANDS.—These islands were known to the ancients as the "Fortunate Isles." The first meridian was referred to the Canary Isles by Hippardrus, about 140 B.C. They were re-discovered by a Norman, named Bethincourt, A.D. 1402; and were seized by the Spaniards, who planted vines, which flourish here, about 1420. The canary bird, so much esteemed in all parts of Europe, is a native of these isles; it was brought into England in 1500.

CAUGHT IN THE RIGGING.—The sailors of the ship have been doing a good stroke of business during the voyage, in consequence of the number of amateurs who mount the rigging, and relieve themselves from the punishment usually inflicted for the offence by the payment of a fee to their capturers. If no payment is immediately made, the gentlemen are bound hand and foot to the rigging, which soon produces the desired effect.

MADEIRA.—So called on account of its woods, it was discovered, it is said, by Mr. Macham, an English gentleman, or mariner, who fled from England for an illicit amour. He was driven here by a storm, and his mistress, a French lady, dying, he made a canoe, and carried the news of his discovery to Pedro, King of Arragon, which occasioned the report that the island was discovered by a Portuguese, A.D. 1345. But it is maintained that the Portuguese did not visit this island until 1419, nor did they colonise it until 1431. It was taken possession of by the British in July, 1801; and again by Admiral Hood and General (now Viscount) Beresford, Dec. 24, 1807, and retained in trust for the royal family of Portugal, which had just then emigrated to the Brazils. It was subsequently restored to the Portuguese crown.

WELL MERITED PUNISHMENT.—On Thursday evening week a passenger was observed to enter into a certain part of the ship devoted and expected to be kept sacred "for the use of ladies only." The door was immediately secured, and the word was passed for a number of A.B.'s to man the pump, the ship's carpenter being at the same time instructed to bore a hole in the roof of the prisoner's apartment of sufficient calibre for the introduction of the nozzle of the hose attached to the pump. All being ready, the men pumped as men will pump who enjoy what they are pumping for, and in a few minutes the man was released, drenched to the skin, and made his way to his berth amidst the laughter of the passengers and crew. It is said that a shower bath is the best cure that has yet been discovered for the complaint under which our hero laboured.

CAPE ST. VINCENT.—A few days ago we passed Cape St. Vincent, famous for the great battles fought here on the 16th of June, 1693, and the 14th of February, 1797. In the former Admiral Rooke, with twenty ships of war, and the Turkish fleet under his convoy, was attacked by Admiral Tourville, with a force vastly superior to his own, off Cape St. Vincent, when twelve English and Dutch men-of-war, and eighty merchantmen, were captured or destroyed by the French. The other battle was one of the most glorious achievements of the British navy. Sir John Jervis, being in command of the Mediterranean fleet of fifteen sail, and gave battle to the Spanish fleet of twenty-seven ships of the line off this cape, and signally defeated the enemy, nearly double in strength, taking four ships, and destroying several others.

---

THE CAPTAIN'S REPORT.

---

*To the Passengers of the Ship Marco Polo.*
LADIES AND GENTLEMEN,

We are enjoying, in many respects, a most remarkable sea voyage. It is not attended as yet by any symptoms of being a speedy one, but there is much reason to hope that the Marco Polo will yet do justice to the high character she bears at home. We are now within the Tropics, and the Surgeon's Report will inform you that the great increase of heat has been the cause of several cases of diarrhoea; otherwise the ship may be considered very healthy. I would recommend that attention be paid to the necessary change of clothing suitable to the changes of latitude. I am glad to bear witness to your constant study in the art and daily practise in the lesson of amusing each other. You have my best wishes.—Yours, faithfully,

WILLIAM WILD
Friday Morning.

**THE MARCO POLO CHRONICLE:**

## A WEEKLY JOURNAL OF EVENTS
ARISING DURING A VOYAGE FROM LIVERPOOL TO AUSTRALIA.

SATURDAY, AUGUST 19, 1854.

### WHAT WE ARE DOING ON BOARD
### THE MARCO POLO.

A FANCY DRESS BALL, on shipboard, in the broad Atlantic, with the thermometer at 89 in the shade, is a freak of fancy of rather a daring character. The proposition was in itself novel; the result was most satisfactory. We require no greater proof of the determination of the passengers to enjoy themselves, now we have witnessed a most brilliant Fancy Dress Ball, which was conceived, and brought to an issue within a single week! And this ball was a fancy one to all intents and purposes, the costumes being extremely various, and in many instances very correct. The wonder is how the thing was done, and where the dresses came from. Had a theatrical wardrobe been on board, with full liberty of access thereto, it is a question whether taste could have been better displayed. But no such an appliance was on board, and many of the attendants at the ball had most of their luggage stowed down "full fathom five" in the lower hold.

Nevertheless, we had the ladies in court dresses, as Swiss shepherdesses, and in other modes of attire—very pretty, but not familiar enough to us to describe; whilst the gentlemen appeared as Greeks and Turks, naval officers, men-of-war's men, jockeys, gold diggers, peasants, pirates, Highlanders, brigands, fine old English gentlemen, "Bloomers," and,

indeed, the usual variety of characters that make up a respectable fancy dress ball. There were a few exceptions to the rule, some of the ladies and gentlemen being attired in plain evening dress, and very well they looked,—reminding us, by the force of contrast, of the home we've left behind us. The whole affair passed off with the greatest *eclat*, and well deserves honourable mention in this portion of the MARCO POLO CHRONICLE.

It would be ridiculous in the extremest sense of the word if we were to continually picture life at sea as an example of that height of elysium—lying on a bed of roses; it is not by any means without its attendant disagreeable circumstances; the rose too often conceals very painful thorns. We had the necessity to endure for two or three days after the Fancy Dress Ball—a calm and its unpleasant consequences. The Marco Polo lay, like a huge log, upon the waters, rising and falling with the swell, but making scarcely any perceptible progress towards our destination. With but very few exceptions, the passengers felt what has been well called an "all-overishness," and the usual disposition for fun was scarcely exhibited. Everybody seemed to have an inclination to do nothing, and it is the only thing in which they succeeded in anything like perfection. Ths gentlemen were too lazy to smoke; and the ladies in vain turned over the leaves of the most interesting works of fiction, or tried to work some "love of a pattern" in the everlasting crochet. But, fortunately for all on board, this state of dormancy was ended a by the rising of a breeze on Wednesday evening, which increased to something like a gale on the following day, and was further accompanied by a continuous shower of rain, which cooled the atmosphere in a very great degree. We are now enjoying a tolerably comfortable state of affairs; but we are very sorry to add that the gale, with the aid of which we are making good speed across the waters, is not blowing in that quarter which our anxious captain desires to enable him to make a really successful passage.

---

### THE FANCY DRESS BALL.

The first Fancy Dress Ball on board the Marco Polo came off on Monday night. The poop deck was fitted up with very great taste, and was generally admitted to be a most excellent ball room. A large awning completely covered in the space thus devoted to Terpsichore, the enclosure being made complete at the sides by means of the ship's signal and other flags. The general effect was very striking, and was strictly nautical. At the end of the room opposite the entrances, the railings of the companion descending to the main deck were covered with flags, forming a kind of raised dais, above which was conspicuously placed one of our national flags—the Union Jack; whilst in juxtaposition was placed the tricoloured flag of our faithful ally France. The lighting was not exactly what might be termed brilliant, the ship's lanterns, although well trimmed, being not quite equal to gas, and we should have our character as "impartial and truthful journalists" open to grave doubts if we were to say otherwise. The band was for this particular occasion stationed on the quarter deck instead of the poop deck—where the dancers most do congregate. This part of the vessel was also completely covered in, and added considerably to the comfort of the ladies and gentlemen passing to and

from the ball room and saloon, as well as affording accommodation to a considerable number of interested spectators. The company began to arrive from their respective berths about eight o'clock, and in the course of half an hour there was a numerous array of ladies and gentlemen....

We must give our testimony in favour of the general appropriateness of the costumes and the manner in which the characters were sustained. Some of the gentlemen appeared in evening dress.... The contrast was agreeable. The programmes of the dances (which were printed at office on board) gave the following, as the order of proceedings:—Quadrille, polka, lancers, waltz, schottische, quadrille; polka, waltz, gallope.—supper,—polka, waltz, quadrille, schottische, lancers, gallope, Sir Roger de Cuverley. Those persons who have been in the habit of attending fancy dress balls can picture to themselves the effect of a combination of the representatives of almost every clime threading the mazes of the merry dance; but those who have not had the opportunity of personal attendance must make a liberal draught upon their imaginations, and, like our legislators do with regard to taxation, "add 10 per cent thereon," and they will arrive at a sufficiently satisfactory result. About half-past eleven supper was served in the saloon, the chair and vice-chair being respectively occupied by Messers. Byrn and Clapperton. After the usual loyal toasts had been given and duly honoured, the toast of the evening, to the health and many happy returns of the birthday of J. Mackay, Jun., Esq., in whose honour the ball was got up, was given from the chair, and was feelingly responded to. Subsequently, the healths of Captain and Mrs. Wild, the patron and patroness of the ball; "the Press," coupled with the health of Mr. F. W. Robinson, the editor and publisher of the MARCO POLO CHRONICLE. Each of these toasts were acknowledged in suitable terms. The repast provided included a liberal variety of delicacies, and the wines were of high character,—the Champagne and Hock being especially "fizzing." The stewards, at all times attentive, were particularly so upon this occasion; After the supper, in accordance with the programme, dancing was renewed, and we may say, in conclusion, that the dancers were "tripping it on the light fantastic toe" as late as five o'clock on Tuesday morning.

---

### MISCELLANEOUS MATTERS.

---

THE HEALTH OF THE PASSENGERS.— There is no sickness on board, with the exception of a few cases of sea sickness.

STARTLING INCIDENT.—Last night, about half-past nine o'clock, a vessel passed us in the reverse direction, rather too near to be agreeable. She had no light at her bow, and apparently no man on the look out, for an unsuccessful attempt was made to speak her.

WHAT THEY EAT AT MELBOURNE.— There are good fish to be had in the Melbourne market; at the Royal we had occasionally a sort of perch broiled for breakfast, which was very good. Pork is also served in its usual forms, though it is not so much eaten as beef and mutton, and costs more. The vegetables I saw in the market looked well, particularly the cauliflowers. There were enormous carrots, nearly a yard long, and stout in proportion. The onions were oblong; squeezed, perhaps into that shape in growing through the adhesive soil. There were also huge potatoes from New Zealand and Adelaide, but they were seldom free from the rot. The few turkeys and fowl did not promise much. Wild duck and other game fowl were often hawked in the streets. I remember seeing a boy with a brace of black swans. But almost everything, animal as well as vegetable, of native growth, has some little oddity about its shape, as if it had run wild in this new continent. Oysters, such as only Englishmen could eat, were hawked in and eaten raw from baskets, at six shillings or more per dozen! Even the shrimp, sold at five shillings a quart, had a young lobster look. I saw frequently oppossums brought in on the shoulders of sports-men. They resemble racoons, only that they are smaller and grayish. If the inhabitants can ever persuade themselves to eat what Frenchmen eat, they may procure from the great swamps and marshes an ample supply of frogs, which are said to grow in these locations almost as large and loud-voiced as those our New York emigrants will be catching and broiling them. Their gourmand fellow-citizens at home have long esteemed frogs very delicate and chicken-like food.—*Peck's Melbourne and the Chincha Islands....*

# A WEEKLY JOURNAL OF EVENTS
### ARISING DURING A VOYAGE FROM LIVERPOOL TO AUSTRALIA.

## SATURDAY, AUGUST 26, 1854.

### WHAT WE ARE DOING ON BOARD
### THE MARCO POLO.

Most of our readers have now got a more correct idea of "a life on the ocean wave," and "a home on the rolling deep," than ever the spirit of inquiry obtained for them in their homes on *terra firma*.

It is a very nice thing in its way; very jolly, somewhat luxurious, and tolerably exciting. But, after all, it must be admitted that it is rather too tedious to be excessively agreeable. Persons of an active and industrious disposition soon become surfeited with even a round of pleasure; and fancy dress balls, concerts, and all the other modes of amusement which have been adopted for the purpose of killing time, become "flat, stale, and unprofitable," when they are unaccompanied by the knowledge that we are making fair progress towards our destination. We can well imagine a glorious ball or concert with the Marco Polo making twelve miles an hour, as surely as we can picture to ourselves a vain attempt to be merry in a dead calm, or two or three knot breeze. Nay, we could believe in the possibility of the passengers being all alive, with a desperate inclination for kicking, if it were blowing great guns—provided that the great guns were pointing in the direction of Melbourne. During the last week we have had sufficient cause to be gloomy,—at least such of us as are anxious for a speedy passage,—for the winds instead of favouring our progress seemed

to forbid it. Everybody was asking everybody when there was a probability of "crossing the line," and nobody could tell. We were informed, for our consolation, both by Captain WILD and his good-tempered and efficient chief officer Mr. CRUICKSHANK that the wind was "right in our teeth," and that the course they were obliged to steer was taking us in the direction of South America; but that probably we might meet with a wind which would carry us over the Equator. Fortunately we fell in with the south-east trade winds on Wednesday, and during Thursday night we crossed the line, thus completing about one-third of our passage out, and we are assured the most difficult portion thereof. We may now expect that our progress will be more rapid than has yet been the case, and consequently mirth and good humour will be again in the ascendant; indeed, we feel assured that the next few weeks will be rife with materials for the MARCO POLO CHRONICLE.

We have made allusion to our "crossing the line" during Thursday night, a consummation so devoutly wished by all our readers, and we have elsewhere detailed the humourous proceedings connected with the time-honoured visit of Neptune and his spouse Amphitrite. We were glad that the whole affair went off with the utmost good humour, and that the proceedings did not go beyond a good joke. The disgraceful scenes which have been recorded as having taken place on board both men-of-war and merchant ships in years gone by naturally led us to the conclusion that with regard to the ceremony of crossing the line, if carried out in its integrity, it is, like many other ancient abuses, a custom far more honoured in the breach than the observance. Neptune has, however, like "his children," as he is pleased to term the good folks on board, become much more civilised, and he is, on the whole, a very respectable and civil old gentleman, considering that the school-master was most certainly abroad when he ought to have finished his education. We rather fancy it was an oversight on the part of his entertainers, that Neptune was not shown the MARCO POLO CHRONICLE Office; he would surely have thought it a new, strange, and satisfactory "sign of the times."...

---

MISCELLANEOUS MATTERS.

---

LETTERS FOR HOME!—A day or two ago, "in the dead waste and middle of the night," a wag called out through one of the hatchways that the passengers were to bring up their letters! Several persons took it for granted that means were at hand for despatching their epistles homewards, and a rush was made up the companion *en dishabille* for the purpose of handing them over They were, as may well be believed, much chagrined to find that they had been "sold."...

POLICE INTELLIGENCE.—Tuesday, August 22.—Before Justice Wild.—John Birkett, landlord of the Marco Polo Grog Stores, Lower Deck, was charged with harbouring disorderly characters about his establishment, contrary to the statute in that case made and provided. Detective Cruickshank stated the nature of the charge. "He was on duty," &c. Mr. Birkett pleaded guilty to the charge, but considered that there were extenuating circumstances, which ought to be taken into consideration, to the effect that water was an element so valuable that he could not afford to reduce the strength of the liquor to any reasonable or drinkable condition, the consequence of which

was that his customers got "half seas over " when they were under the impression that they had not "crossed the line." Defendant was cautioned, had his retail license suspended for a week, and was ordered to pay costs.

DRUNK, AND VERY DISORDERLY.—On Monday night, somewhere about eight o'clock, the passengers generally were startled out of their propriety by hearing a scuffle on the lower deck, which was shortly afterwards renewed on the quarter deck. We have obtained the following particulars relating to the affair. It appears that a man named John Dooley, an Irishman, a passenger in the intermediate cabin, went to the store room and requested to be supplied with some whiskey, which Mr. Birkett (the purser) refused to supply, the man being then in a state of intoxication. Upon being refused the whiskey, Dooley made use of some insolent language, and, upon being remonstrated with, he made a blow at the head of Mr. Birkett with a metal teapot, and became otherwise so violent, that by the orders of Mr. Cruickshank (the chief mate) he was handcuffed, and taken before Captain Wild. As soon as he reached the quarter deck he observed the captain, at whom he at once aimed a blow with his manacled and clenched hands, which fortunately did not take effect. We shall not defile our columns with a single example of the horrid oaths and imprecations which were uttered under the influence of drink by a man who is said to be, *when sober,* "quiet and well conducted." Dooley was kept in irons all night, and on the following morning, having expressed his sorrow for what he had done, and begged the captain's pardon, he was discharged.

THE MOTLEYS OF MELBOURNE.—When it is remembered that every building, hut, and tent was crowded with tenants, it may be imagined how animated the principal streets of the business parts of Melbourne appeared to a "new chum" just from a long, lonely voyage. Collins-street, as I passed down it the first morning, was as thronged as Broadway. I stopped on the Elizabeth-street corner and took an observation. Long teams of as many as twenty yoke of bullocks to each, were drawing single waggons up and down giving one a not too favourable impression with regard to the state of the roads out of the town. Rough horses, the roughest and shabbiest that can be conceived, were cantering to and fro, ridden by men with long boots, stuck far into short stirrups, and who seemed to urge their forlorn beasts along by jumping in their saddles and elevating their elbows. Heavy chaise-carts and dog-carts, horse-killing vehicles, unknown in the United States, ponies with errand-boys, and dray-carts with veteran hacks, in the last stages of decline, filled up the middle of the street. Upon the side-walk was a motley throng, all with busy faces and "speculation" in their eye; a few clean and well-dressed, in the English fashion, Melbourne exquisites; the major part a mixture of jockey and farmer, with long boots or gaiters, and loaded whips; merchants with eager and calculating eyes; Jews of all nations and combinations; swells of low degree; Parsees and Chinese, sportsmen, a few well-dressed ladies, in long skirts draggled with mud; servant-girls and such, policemen in blue uniform, escorts in ditto, with white facing; now and then a soldier and so on down to the unshorn, unwashed, almost undressed rabble, whether composed of disappointed diggers, or what, I know not, but exhibiting some of the lowest and dirtiest specimens I ever saw in my life. There was, at least so I fancied, a head-strong, reckless energy of movement in everything. I seemed to feel as if a great stream of life were dashing by in a torrent, loud, violent, impetuous, uncontrollable. It was impossible not to be susceptible to the sympathetic influences of the scene. Though I had no hope of making money, and consequently nothing directly in common with the throng of wealth-seekers, and was indeed occupied by much more vexing cares, I could not help feeling a sort of factitious vitality.—*Peck's Melbourne and the Chincha Islands.*

## POET'S CORNER.

### Meeting at Sea

As ships from their respective ports,
  To distant harbours sailing on,
Meet with each other on the deep,
  And hail, and answer, and are gone
So we upon the sea of life
  Have met, as mortals often will;
One from the prairies of the West,
  One from the land of rock and hill.
So we shall pass our various ways,
  As vessels parting on the main,
And in the years to came our paths
  May never meet nor cross again.
Yet when life's voyage all is done,
  *Where'er apart our paths may tend,*
*We'll drop our anchors side by side,*
*In the same* HAVEN *at the end.*

GEO. B. HIGGINBOTHAM,
Assistant Surgeon, Marco Polo.
August 25,1854.

### THE CAPTAIN'S REPORT.

*To the Passengers of the Ship Marco Polo.*
LADIES AND GENTLEMEN,
    You will be rejoiced to hear that we are now making very creditable progress in our passage towards Melbourne. We have passed the Rubicon, and I anticipate but little further difficulty during the few remaining weeks which I shall have the pleasure of meeting you on board the Marco Polo. I think that it is extremely possible that you may be landed in Melbourne in the course of the next six or seven weeks. I am glad to hear from the Surgeons of the ship that notwithstanding the recent hot weather that your general health continues very good; I hope sincerely that it may continue so, and that I may, in due course land you safe and sound at your destination.— Yours truly,
    WILLIAM WILD.
    Saturday Morning.

# GLOSSARY

More detailed descriptions of many of these terms can be found in *The Oxford Companion to Ships and the Sea* (see bibliography).

**Adze** An axe-like tool with a curved blade set at right angles to the handle. A principal shipbuilder's tool used for shaping wooden beams, knees, and planks.

**Alluvial** Made up of an accumulation of earth or sand deposited by flowing water from a creek or river.

**Auger** A hand tool used for boring holes in wood, usually of an exact diameter and depth.

**Ballast** Any heavy material placed in the hold of a ship to provide stability and prevent capsizing. A ship carrying ballast is said to be "in ballast."

**Barque** *or* **Bark** A vessel having three masts with the mast furthest aft (mizzen) fore-and-aft rigged and the others square rigged.

**Barquentine** *or* **Barkenteen** A small bark, usually with three masts, with its foremast square rigged and the others (main and mizzen) fore-and-aft rigged.

**Beam ends** Literally the ends of a ship's transverse beams. A ship over on its beam ends is over on its side so that its deck beams are nearly vertical.

**Bilge** The lowest part of a ship's hull, below where its shape changes from nearly vertical to nearly horizontal. The term bilge is used to refer to both the inside and the outside of the ship.

**Binnacle** A box, usually placed near the wheel, containing the ship's compass.

**Block** A massive wooden support for the keel of a vessel during its construction.

**Boatswain** *or* **bo'sun** The ship's officer responsible for the sails, rigging, anchors, cables, etc.

**Boom** A pole or spar run out from a mast and attached to the base of a sail.

**Bow port**  An opening made in the hull close to the bow of a timber carrier to permit the loading and unloading of long lengths of timber directly into and out of its cargo space.

**Bowsprit**  A large spar projecting forward above the bow allowing sail to be set far forward.

**Brig**  A vessel with two square rigged masts widely used for coastal trading.

**Brigantine**  A two-masted vessel, square rigged on its foremast, like a brig, and fore-and-aft rigged on its main, like a schooner.

**Capstan**  A device placed on the deck and used to provide a mechanical advantage for lifting heavy items such as sails and anchors. It is composed of a cylinder turned around its vertical axis by workers pushing on horizontal bars inserted into it. A rope or chain with its end attached to the item to be moved is wound around the cylinder in that way.

**Ceiling**  A layer of planks running lengthwise, fastened to the inside surface of the frames of the hull to the level of the beams.

**Chafing gear**  Material put on rigging, masts, and yards to prevent abrasion by rubbing.

**Chandler**  The ship's chandler was its supplier of provisions.

**Coaming**  A raised edge around a ship's hatch to prevent water from entering.

**Cutter**  In the days of sail, a fast, small vessel usually with one mast and rigged like a sloop.

**Deal**  A length of timber sawn from a log at least six feet long.

**Dowel**  A thin cylinder of wood, a peg, used to fasten two or more pieces of wood together.

**Draft**  A line on a ship's hull designating the depth of water it displaces.

**Draw knife**  A cutting tool with a blade and a handle at both ends used to shape wood by drawing it towards the user.

**Ends**  The fore and aft extremities of the ship.

**Entrance**  The part of the ship that first cleaves the water as it moves ahead.

**Fastenings**  Broadly used to identify nails or pegs holding pieces of the ship together such as planks to frames. These were usually made of iron, copper or wood.

**Fathom**  Six feet.

**Figurehead**  A carved work of art, usually a bust or figure, placed on the bow of the ship beneath the bowsprit.

**Fittings**  Fixtures, furnishings, and decorations for the ship.

**Fore-and-aft sails**  Sails which, when at rest, hang in the long (fore-and-aft) axis of the vessel. Square sails, in contrast, hang from transverse yards.

**Forecastle** *or* **foc's'le** *or* **fo'c's'le**  The forward part of the ship containing the sailors' quarters.

**Frame**  One of the ribs of the skeleton of a wooden ship, made of pieces of wood assembled together. Typically, frames are U-shaped and are fixed at a right angle to the keel at the bottom of the U and the side rail at the top. Frames give the basic shape to the hull of the ship. The word frame can also be used to refer collectively to the entire skeleton of the ship.

**Halyard**  A rope or tackle used to raise or lower a sail or flag.

**Hand plane**  A carpenter's tool pushed by hand to smooth and straighten the surface of wood by removing shavings from it.

**Hogging**  An arching upwards of the keel and adjacent hull of the ship amidships. Hogging was a common problem for wooden sailing ships because they were more buoyant amidships than at their heavier ends.

**Iron founder**  One who casts iron, in this case into nails and ship's fittings.

**Keel**  The backbone of the hull formed by a longitudinal timber on which the entire structure of the hull is built. The keel is the lowermost structure of the hull.

**Keelson**  A longitudinal timber placed internal to the keel and bolted to it. The keelson helps to secure the frames and the masts.

**Knee**  A piece of metal or wood with a right-angle bend used to provide support at the places where the ship's timbers intersect. In particular, knees fasten the ship's transverse beams to its frames.

**Landfall**  The first sighting of land after a sea voyage.

**Lighters**  Open barges used to ferry cargo back and forth to ships unable to dock because the water at the dock is too shallow for them.

**Mainsail**  On a square rigged ship like *Marco Polo*, the ship's principal sail carried on the mainmast.

**Mall or maul**  A wooden mallet.

**Mizzen or mizen**  On a ship with two or three masts, the mast closest to the stern.

**Oakum**  Fibre used for caulking and obtained by unwinding ropes typically made from hemp or manila.

**Packet**  A ship on a regular schedule between ports, carrying cargo, passengers, and mail.

**Pilaster**  A pillar or column, rectangular or square in cross section and often projecting from a wall.

**Placer mining**  The mining of deposits of gravel or sand laid down by flowing water or glaciers for particles or nuggets of metals such as gold.

**Plank**  A long, flat, smooth piece of wood. Planks were used to line both the inner and outer surfaces of the frames. In the latter location they formed the outer skin of the ship and in the former, its ceiling.

**Poop**  A structure above the flush weather deck, towards the stern of the vessel.

**Rider and sister keelsons**  Additional long timbers fastened next to the keelson.

**Rigging**  The set of ropes or chains used to support the masts, manage the yards, and work the sails.

**Royal sail**  A small sail set on the mast above the topgallant sail.

**Run**  The underwater part of the hull, aft.

**Scarph *or* scarf**  A longitudinal overlapping joint between two pieces of wood of the same thickness.

**Schooner**  A small vessel, fore-and-aft rigged, with two or more masts and one or more topsails. Used for coasting, fishing off the Grand Banks of Newfoundland, and sometimes for racing.

**Sharp**  Refers to a ship with a keen edge forward, to slice through the water more easily.

**Sheer**  The upward curve of the upper portion of the hull towards the bow and stern as seen from the side.

**Sheerlegs**  A device made of two or three spars lashed together at the top and used for hoisting anything heavy, especially large pieces of timber.

**Ship**  Specifically, a square-rigged, sea-going vessel with three masts and a bowsprit.

**Ship's skeleton**  The vessel without its outer layer of planking, displaying its frames.

**Sloop**  A small vessel with a single mast, fore-and-aft rigged. Differs from a cutter in that it has a fixed bowsprit.

**Snow**  A large (up to one thousand tons) two-masted merchant vessel with masts and yards similar to a brig.

**Spar deck**  An upper deck on which spare masts, yards, etc. are stored.

**Spokeshave**  A carpenter's tool used for shaping and finishing spokes and other shapes of wood.

**Square-rigged**  A vessel is said to be square rigged when its main source of propulsion is from four-sided sails set from yards slung transversely from its masts.

**Stem**  The upright timber at the bow of the vessel, bolted to the keel, to which the planks are fastened.

**Sternpost**  The upright timber at the stern of the vessel, bolted to the keel, which supports the rudder.

**Stocks**  Collectively, the huge blocks of wood on which the keel of the ship is laid and the ship is supported while it is being built.

**Stud sail** *or* **studdingsail**  A sail set outside the reach of a working sail to extend the canvas area, usually in light winds.

**Tail-race**  A wooden conduit built to channel flowing water containing the diggings from a mine.

**Topgallant**  The sail above the topsail and below the royal on a square-rigged ship.

**Treenails**  Wooden (usually oak) pegs or dowels used to join wooden parts of the ship. Treenails could be hammered tightly into place and, unlike iron spikes, did not corrode.

**Ways**  A parallel wooden track built to guide the ship's cradle into the water during launching.

**Windlass**  A mechanical device consisting of a drum or cylinder on a horizontal axle. A rope or chain is wound on the drum and used to lift heavy objects such as the ship's anchor.

**Windmill pump**  A water pump driven by the force of the wind on sails or vanes attached to a revolving shaft.

**Yard**  A spar slung from a mast and crossing it horizontally and used to support a sail.

# SELECTED BIBLIOGRAPHY

## ARCHIVAL SOURCES

Archives Office of Tasmania, Letter Series NS1543, Wilkinson Family Papers.

Correspondence of J. M. Whelan. Courtesy of Dr. M. T. Shortall, County Down, Northern Ireland.

Correspondence of Elbridge White. Courtesy of Sandra Hume, Montague, Prince Edward Island.

Diary of William Culshaw Greenhalgh, National Museums Liverpool (Merseyside Maritime Museum), Maritime Archive and Library, Reference DX/1676.

La Trobe Australian Manuscripts Collection, State Library of Victoria, Melbourne.

Mitchell Library, State Library of New South Wales, Sydney.
National Library of Australia, Canberra.

## BOOKS

Andrewes, William J. H., ed. *The Quest for Longitude*. Cambridge, Massachusetts: Harvard University Press, 1996.

Armour, Charles A., and Thomas Lackey. *Sailing Ships of the Maritimes: An Illustrated History of Shipping and Shipbuilding in the Maritime Provinces of Canada, 1750–1925*. Toronto: McGraw-Hill Ryerson, 1975.

Backman, Brian, and Phil Backman. *Bluenose*. Toronto: McClelland and Stewart, 1965.

Baillie, G. H., C. Clutton, and C. A. Ilbert. *Britten's Old Clocks and Watches and their Makers*. 7th ed. New York: Bonanza Books, 1956.

Barrett, Charles, ed. *Gold in Australia*. Melbourne: Cassell and Company, 1951.

Chapelle, Howard I. *The Search for Speed Under Sail, 1700–1855*. New York: Bonanza Books, 1967.

Charlwood, Don. *The Long Farewell*. London: Allen Lane, 1981.

Copland, James. *A Dictionary of Practical Medicine*. London: Longman, Brown, Green, Longmans, & Roberts, 1858.

Crothers, William L. *The American-Built Clipper Ship 1850–1856, Characteristics, Construction, and Details*. Camden, Maine: International Marine, 1996.

Cutler, Carl C. *Greyhounds of the Sea, The Story of the American Clipper Ship*. Annapolis, Maryland: United States Naval Institute, 1930.

Druett, Joan. *Rough Medicine: Surgeons at Sea in the Age of Sail*. New York: Routledge, 2000.

Friedenberg, Zachary B. *Medicine Under Sail*. Annapolis, Maryland: Naval Institute Press, 2002.

Gardiner, Robert, ed. *Sail's Last Century: The Merchant Sailing Ship, 1830–1930*. London: Conway Maritime Press, 1993.

Greenhill, Basil. *The Evolution of the Wooden Ship*. New York: Facts on File, 1988.

Haines, Robin. *Life and Death in the Age of Sail: The Passage to Australia*.

Sydney: University of New South Wales Press, 2003.

Hollett, David. *Fast Passage to Australia*. London: Fairplay Publications, 1986.

———. *Passage to the New World*. Abergaveny, England: P. M. Heaton, 1995.

Kemp, Peter. *The Oxford Companion to Ships and the Sea*. London: Oxford University Press, 1976.

Koskie, Jack L. *Ships that Shaped Australia*. London: Angus and Robertson, 1987.

Lloyd, Christopher, and Jack Coulter. *Medicine and the Navy, 1200–1900*. Vol. 4 *1815–1900*. Edinburgh and London: E. & S. Livingstone, 1963.

Lubbock, Basil. *The Colonial Clippers*. Glasgow: Brown, Son and Ferguson, Nautical Publishers, 1975.

MacGregor, David R. *British and American Clippers: A Comparison of their Design, Construction, and Performance in the 1850s*. London: Conway Maritime Press, 1993.

———. *Fast Sailing Ships: Their Design and Construction, 1775–1875*. Lymington, Hampshire: Nautical Publishing, 1973.

———. *Merchant Sailing Ships, 1850–1875: Heyday of Sail*. London: Conway Maritime Press and Lloyd's of London Press, 1984.

McCalman, Iain, Alexander Cook, and Andrew Reeves, eds. *Gold: Forgotten Histories and Lost Objects of Australia*. Cambridge: Cambridge University Press, 2001.

Place, Marian T. *Gold Down Under*. London: Crowell-Collier Press, 1969.

Sobel, Dava, and William J. H. Andrewes. *The Illustrated Longitude*. New York: Penguin Studio, 1998.

Spicer, Stanley T. *Masters of Sail: The Era of Square-rigged Vessels in the Maritime Provinces*. Toronto: Ryerson Press, 1968.

Stammers, Michael K. *The Passage Makers*. Brighton, Sussex: Toredo Books, 1978.

Stephens, David E. *W. D. Lawrence: The Man and the Ship*. Hantsport, Nova Scotia: Lancelot Press, 1975.

Vroom, Richard, and Arthur Doyle. *Old New Brunswick: A Victorian Portrait*. Toronto: Oxford University Press, 1978.

Wallace, Frederick W. *In the Wake of the Wind-Ships: Notes, Records and Biographies Pertaining to the Square-Rigged Merchant Marine of British North America*. New York: George Sully and Company, 1927.

Wallace, Frederick W. *Wooden Ships and Iron Men: The Story of the Square-Rigged Merchant Marine of British North America, the Ships, their Builders and Owners, and the Men Who Sailed Them.* London and Toronto: Hodder and Stoughton, 1924.

Wilson, Garth. *A History of Shipbuilding and Naval Architecture in Canada.* Ottawa: National Museum of Science and Technology, 1994.

Winchester, Clarence. *Shipping Wonders of the World: A Saga of the Sea in Story and Picture.* Vol. 2. London: The Fleetway House, 1937.

Woolcock, Helen R. *Rights of Passage.* London and New York: Tavistock Publications, 1986.

Wright, Esther Clark. *Saint John Ships and Their Builders.* Wolfville, Nova Scotia: privately printed, 1975.

## WEBSITES

Amos Crosby & Marco Polo. http://www.yarmcentral.ednet.ns.ca/sailing_ships/marco_polo/marco_polo.htm

Shipworm.
http://www.bartleby.com/65/sh/shipworm.html

Measles History.
http://www.cdc.gov/nip/diseases/measles/history.htm

Measles Initiative.
http://www.measlesinitiative.org/index3.asp

Saint John, New Brunswick.
http://new-brunswick.net/Saint_John/vintage.html

The Era of the Clipper Ships by Donald Gunn Ross III.
http://www.eraoftheclipperships.com/eraweb.html

The First Payable Goldfield Found in Australia (Ophir).
http://www.users.tpg.com.au/dtdan//ophir.htm

The History of the Sextant.
http://www.mat.uc.pt/~helios/Mestre/Novemboo/H61iflan.htm

The Marco Polo Project in Saint John, New Brunswick.
http://new-brunswick.net/marcopolo/index.html

Gerardus Mercator. http://www-gap.dcs.st-and.ac.uk/~history/Mathematicians/Mercator_Gerardus.html

# IMAGE SOURCES

**Figure 1** *(pg vi)* From Jack L. Koskie, *Ships that Shaped Australia* (London: Angus and Robertson, 1987), 67. Courtesy of Mrs. Jack Koskie.

**Figure 2** *(pg 9)* Courtesy of the Provincial Archives of New Brunswick. P11-20.

**Figure 3** *(pg 9)* Notman Photographic Archives, McCord Museum of Canadian History, Montreal. View-3267 Harbour, Saint John, NB, ca. 1898. Courtesy of the McCord Museum of Canadian History, Montreal.

**Figure 4** *(pg 11)* Courtesy of the New Brunswick Museum, (1945.762).

**Figure 5** *(pg 15)* From Basil Greenhill, *The Evolution of the Wooden Ship* (New York: Facts on File, 1988), 89. Courtesy of Sam Manning, Camden, Maine.

**Figures 6 & 7** *(pg 17)* Courtesy of The Mariners' Museum, Newport News, Virginia.

**Figure 8** *(pg 19)* From Greenhill, *The Evolution Of The Wooden Ship*, 102. Courtesy of Sam Manning, Camden, Maine.

**Figure 9** *(pg 20)* Courtesy of Sam Manning, Camden, Maine.

**Figure 10** *(pg 20)* Courtesy of the Provincial Archives of New Brunswick. P210-2765.

**Figure 11** *(pg 23)* Courtesy of the Provincial Archives of New Brunswick. P5-361.

**Figure 12** *(pg 23)* Courtesy of the New Brunswick Museum (12996).

**Figure 13** *(pg 28)* Courtesy of the Yarmouth County Museum and Archives.

**Figure 14** *(pg 30)* From *The Illustrated London News*, February 19, 1853. With thanks to the University of British Columbia Library.

**Figure 15** *(pg 35)* Courtesy of La Trobe Picture Collection, State Library of Victoria.

**Figure 16** *(pg 40)* From Michael K. Stammers, *The Passage Makers* (Brighton, Sussex: Toredo Books, 1978), 44. Courtesy of National Museums Liverpool (Merseyside Maritime Museum).

**Figure 17** *(pg 55)* From *The Illustrated London News*, July 10, 1852. With thanks to the University of British Columbia Library.

**Figure 18** *(pg 55)* From *The Australasian Sketcher*, December 18, 1880. Courtesy of the National Library of Australia. Bib ID 2556753.

**Figure 19** *(pg 58)* From *The Illustrated London News*, February 12, 1887. With thanks to the University of British Columbia Library.

**Figure 20** *(pg 61)* From *The Illustrated London News*, July 10, 1852. With thanks to the University of British Columbia Library.

**Figure 21** *(pg 61)* From *The Illustrated London News*, April 13, 1844. With thanks to the University of British Columbia Library.

**Figure 22** *(pg 67)* From *The Illustrated London News*, April 13, 1844. With thanks to the University of British Columbia Library.

**Figure 23** *(pg 71)* Courtesy of Jim Stackhouse, Saint John, New Brunswick.

**Figure 24** *(pg 79)* From *The Illustrated London News*, February 12, 1887. With thanks to the University of British Columbia Library.

**Figure 25** *(pg 85)* From *The Illustrated London News*, February 12, 1887. With thanks to the University of British Columbia Library.

**Figure 26** *(pg 96)* Courtesy of Captain C. (Bud) Robinson, Tobermory, Ontario.

**Figure 27** *(pg 102)* From *The Illustrated London News*, February 12, 1887. With thanks to the University of British Columbia Library.

**Figure 28** *(pg 103, back cover)* From Don Charlwood, *The Long Farewell* (London: Allen Lane, 1981), 22. Courtesy of Don Charlwood, Warrandyte, Victoria.

**Figure 29** *(pg 109)* Courtesy of Peter Ifland, Cincinnati, Ohio, author of *Taking the Stars: Celestial Navigation from Argonauts to Astronauts*.

**Figure 30** *(pg 111)* Reproduced by kind permission of Pieces of Time, 1–7 Davies Mews, London W1Y 2LP; www.antique-watch.com.

**Figure 31** *(pg 119)* Courtesy of the New Brunswick *Telegraph-Journal*.

# INDEX